LEFT BEHIND

Peter & Patti Lalonde

HARVEST HOUSE PUBLISHERS
Eugene, Oregon 97402

Scripture quotations in this book are taken from the King James Version of the Bible.

LEFT BEHIND

Copyright © Ontario #1006094 and Ontario #1006095
Published by Harvest House Publishers
Eugene, Oregon 97402

Library of Congress Cataloging-in-Publication Data

Lalonde, Peter.
    Left behind / Peter and Patti Lalonde.
        p. cm.
    ISBN 1-56507-364-9 (alk. paper)
    1. Rapture (Christian eschatology). 2. Second Advent. 3. Bible—Prophecies—
Eschatology. 4. Christian life. I. Lalonde, Patti, 1959-   . II. Title.
BT887.L35 1995   95-17524
236'.9—dc20   CIP

Printed in the United States of America.

95   96   97   98   99   00   01   02   —   10   9   8   7   6   5   4   3   2   1

CONTENTS

CHAPTER ONE

A LETTER TO THE OTHER SIDE

Dear Friend:

Hello. My name is Peter Lalonde. My wife, Patti, and I wanted to write this letter to try to help you understand the world in which you are living.

This is a very difficult letter for us to write because we are separated from you by an event so extraordinary that it has literally changed both you and us forever. Indeed, as we sit here and write these words to you in the mid-1990s, the event you have witnessed seems so distant to us, so unreal, it is almost impossible for us to even contemplate.

And though you may be reading this letter only weeks or months after we have written it, we are still separated by a chasm of time and space so great that it truly is beyond full human comprehension.

We know these words sound strong. But we also somehow perceive that strong words and direct communication are what you are seeking right now. If we are right, if we can see even darkly into your world, yours is a time of confusion and yet of wonder, unlike anything the greatest Hollywood minds ever put on screen.

We can't pretend to understand this world of yours. We can't begin to fathom the fear, the panic, and (most of all) the loss you must be suffering. We know that if you are reading these words in the moments soon after this great disappearance, chances are that this book was left by someone close to you—someone who loved you and talked to you about this day many times and has now vanished from the very face of the earth . . . maybe right before your eyes!

Again, let us ask. How can we possibly write these words to you? How can we make sense to you when we don't fully understand your world—or even the way in which your mind is now undoubtedly racing over these words? We cannot possibly understand. We cannot possibly find the right words. Fortunately, we have help. Help that you know nothing of. Help that we want to tell you about.

Let Us Tell You About Our World

As we said, we are writing this letter to you in

the mid-1990s. In our minds everything in the world seems to be going along normally. Patti and I live in Canada on the beautiful Niagara Peninsula. The water is going over the mighty falls every day just as it has since its creation. Honeymooners still flock here and everything is routine—or so it would seem.

Many of us sense the impending event that you have now witnessed. Its sound, its feel is in the air. Yet at the same time our minds scoff at the very idea. To us it sounds so improbable, so unreal that we wonder if we have lost our minds.

Think of what we are saying from our point in history. We are saying to an incredulous world, "There is going to be a time of great trial, and then the world as we know it is going to end. But don't worry—before any of that happens, all of us who understand are going to vanish first!" You can imagine what the honeymooners and tourists and the rest of the world thinks of that. After all, everything seems so normal.

Are We Nuts? Or Is the Proof in the Pudding?

Most people think that such ideas are simply spawned from a kind of psychosis as we approach the year 2000. In some ways they are right. The approach to the year 2000 is like a magnet drawing every kook out of the woodwork. Yet there is something more, something distinct from this lunacy.

However, before we talk about all of this, we want to remind you that you are in a very different position from the people hearing about this in our time. Unlike the people in our world, you have something they don't have. You have proof. You *know* that it happened. You are living on the other side. Above all else, don't forget that! Let that simple fact anchor you to the rest of this book.

Remember to hold on tight because there are powerful forces working on your mind, trying to make you believe that what we are telling you is preposterous, trying to make you accept any other explanation. But don't ignore us. The proof is right there before you. What we said would happen, *has!*

Let us make something clear right away. We are not prophets. We are not great seers or psychics who saw this coming. We really don't have any powers at all. We are just a couple who have seen and understood the evidence given by the One who we believe to be the greatest mind in the universe.

That someone is God. And much as we are writing this letter to you, He wrote a book to everyone on earth and called it the Bible. All that we are doing in this book is telling you what He told us in His book.

Maybe you have had a Bible lying around for years. If so, grab it and hold on to it! Virtually every detail of the strange and dangerous world in which you now live is recorded in there. In this letter, we just want to explain some of what is in there and show you where to find it.

The Chain of Evidence

We sit here in our world almost two millennia

after a man named Jesus Christ, who was more than just a man, walked this earth. Why are we so convinced that He is about to "snatch" Patti and me and every person who truly believes in Him off this earth?

That is a fundamental question. And the answer, such as is always the case in the Bible, is really quite simple. You see, Jesus told us that there would be a generation somewhere in time which would see a series of signs. These signs, Jesus said, would be a signal to the generation that would witness the very events you have witnessed—including this great and troubling disappearance of millions of people all over the world.

Jesus and the Hebrew prophets told us that this final generation (that's right—you are now living in the very last part of the very last generation) would begin when Israel returned from worldwide dispersion and persecution to become a nation again. That happened in 1948. That was the first sign.

At the same time the prophets told us we would see the development of weapons so powerful that mankind could literally destroy the entire planet. That was never true until this generation. Bows, arrows, cannons, and even conventional arms never had that power. Today it exists.

Then we were told to watch for a military power to the north of Israel. When no one is expecting it, that great military power will surprise the entire world and attack Israel. Today the Soviet empire is gone. But the weapons are still there. No one fears Russia anymore, but she still possesses the very military arsenal the Bible spoke of. In our world, as in yours, the attack would be a surprise just as the Bible said.

The same generation, we are told, would see the birth of a democratic empire based in Europe that would spread its influence over the whole world. What is today the European Union will become in your day the heart of the most powerful empire in all of human history.

Another thing which identifies our time as a part of the last generation and your time as another is the movement toward peace that seems to be sweeping the world. The Bible told us very clearly that a relative peace would sweep the world in the last days. Unfortunately, it would be a very deceptive peace that would actually lead to the greatest war in history.

There are many other signs (including the birth of a global electronic economy that would make it possible to track the buying and selling done by everyone on earth), but let us just mention one more for the time being.

The Hebrew prophet Daniel, writing about 2500 years ago, told us that this last generation would be unlike any other generation at any time in human history. How would it be different? God told Daniel this "terminal" generation would see such an explosive increase in knowledge that man would literally leap into the future.

You don't need me to tell you how true this has been. Think about it for a minute. Let's say that time travel were possible. Imagine a man being transported from the year 500 B.C. to A.D. 500. How much really changed in those 1000 years? Not that much. Depending upon where you lived, men still lived in houses of stone and cooked over a fire. Or how about a sailor being transported from 400 B.C. to A.D. 1492 when Columbus sailed to the new land? The sailor may not have even known that he had traveled those 2000 years by looking at the engineering of the ships. Nothing really changed. The same held true for much of the world right up until the turn of the twentieth century.

Now think what has happened in the past 80 or so years. We have gone from the Wright brothers to the moon to the space shuttle. We have gone from horse-drawn carriages to Ferraris, and from the Pony Express to CNN and cyberspace.

Computers today are capable of executing millions of instructions per second and are now busily using that processing power to invent even more powerful computers.

These are some of the reasons that Patti and I and thousands of other Christians believe we are living in the last generation before "the great disappearance" and the very specific period of time in which you are now living. We will share many more reasons in the pages ahead, but for now we want to tell you about this time in which you are living and what lies ahead.

You Must Decide

As we mentioned earlier, Patti and I have written this letter before the most dramatic and earth-shattering event in human history to provide you with the strongest evidence possible to illustrate the truth of our explanation for what has taken place. The evidence was simple to find because the Bible told us about the great disappearance. More than that, we knew when it would be close at hand because of the signs the Bible gave. This is very dramatic proof.

However, we want you to understand that you are going to be hearing many other explanations for what has taken place. In fact, we can tell you now that these explanations are going to be so convincing that every fiber of your mind and being is going to tell you they are true. We already have a good idea what some of these explanations will be, and we'll talk about them a little later. But please never forget that we told you this was going to happen. Moreover, don't overlook the fact that we are also going to give a pretty detailed picture of both what is happening right now and what is going to happen in the days ahead. God wants you to know this. He has provided ironclad proof!

CHAPTER TWO

WHO LEFT AND WHERE DID THEY GO?

If you recently witnessed the disappearance of millions of people from the earth, Patti and I have no doubt that you will be confused and probably frightened beyond imagination. Once your initial panic has subsided, you will have a lot of questions. The purpose of this book is to provide you with the best answers we can give about what has happened and about what your future holds. And please believe us: There is hope. There is an explanation. There really is.

Like you, millions of people around the globe will be grieving the loss of loved ones. Like you, they are wondering if it is a blessing or a curse that they were not taken. Were you spared? Or are you missing out on some great and exciting experience? And what is this all about anyway? Take a deep breath, and let's start at the beginning.

Who Left?

This event you have witnessed was predicted very specifically by the Bible. But the Bible also explains that all of those who disappeared shared one thing in common. Whether they were from the United States, Canada, China, Africa, or any other part of the world, they were *all* true Bible-believing Christians.

As two members of that group, we can tell you our beliefs. We believe that Jesus Christ is the Son of God who died on a cross in our place to pay for our sins. We have accepted Him as Lord and Savior. In so doing, we became part of the family of God and that family has just been united in heaven.

There will be many people remaining in the world who call themselves Christians. In the last days leading up to this mass disappearance, known to us as "the rapture," many claimed to be true disciples of Christ. But only those who by faith and with all their heart truly believed that Jesus was the *only* Son of God and was the *only* way to salvation were taken away in this rapture. So by definition, at an instant after this rapture took place, there was not one *true* believer left on the whole planet.

As Patti and I have said before, we want to prove to you that the Bible, that same dusty old book that probably lay around your house for years, is indeed the most relevant book in your world. Through it God told us all about the world in which you are living.

So let's get started. You will not find the word *rapture* itself in the Bible (and we urge you to immediately try to find a Bible and start reading it). How did we come up with this name? In 1 Thessalonians 4:17 the Bible says that Christians will be "caught up" to meet the Lord in the air. Greek was the original language in which this passage was written, and the translation of "caught up" is *harpazo*. It is from *raptos*, the Latin derivative of *harpazo*, that Christians came up with the name "rapture."

Even though the word *rapture* is not in the Bible, a description of the event certainly can be found there. The Bible foretold that this event would definitely take place. Let's look at a few places in Scripture that will show you where Jesus made a promise to Christians that He would come back for them and take them to be with Him. The first Scripture we want to look at can be found in John 14:1-3:

> Let not your heart be troubled; ye believe in God, believe also in me. In my Father's house are many mansions; if it were not so, I would have told you. I go to prepare a place for you. And if I go and prepare a place for you, I will come again, and receive you unto myself; that where I am, there ye may be also.

The disciples of Jesus had been concerned that He, nearly 2000 years ago, was going to leave them.

Jesus is telling them in this passage that He must go, but He gave them a promise that He would come again one day and gather all believers to Himself. This promise was intended for *all* believers in Him. And this is exactly what has taken place with the disappearance of millions of people from the earth.

If you think about it for a moment, you will realize that there were those who believed in Jesus in every century since He was on earth. That means that most of the believers were not alive in our day. Most had died (or as the Bible says, fallen asleep). So, this group that Jesus gathered during the rapture was made up of those who had died and those who were still alive when He came. This means that what you have just witnessed was a resurrection of the dead, which you could not see, and a catching up of the living, which you could! The Bible told us all about this long ago:

> For this we say unto you by the word of the Lord, that we which are alive and remain unto the coming of the Lord shall not prevent them which are asleep. For the Lord himself shall descend from heaven with a shout, with the voice of the archangel, and with the trump of God, and the dead in Christ shall rise first. Then we which are alive and remain shall be caught up together with them in the clouds to meet the Lord in the air, and so shall we ever be with the Lord (1 Thessalonians 4:15-17).

The Rapture Is a Mystery

One of the foremost Christian teachers on biblical events during our present point in history is Hal Lindsey. Appropriately, he wrote a book titled simply *The Rapture.* In it he explained this resurrection that you have witnessed:

> In I Corinthians, Chapter 15, the apostle Paul, under the inspiration of God's Spirit, is teaching about the certainty of every believer's resurrection from the dead. He also reveals that the resurrection body will be wonderfully changed into an eternal immortal form that has real substance.
>
> Paul clearly teaches that our new body will "bear the image of the heavenly," that is, like the Lord Jesus' resurrected body (Verse 49). In this regard, he says, "Flesh and blood cannot inherit the kingdom of God; nor does the perishable inherit the imperishable" (Verse 50). In other words, our present body of flesh and blood, which must be sustained by elements of the earth which are perishable, must be changed to another form. This new form has material being, but it is of a kind that is suited for the spiritual, imperishable, eternal atmosphere of heaven. . . .
>
> One thing, however, is necessary to be resurrected: We must first die! Resurrection is only for the dead. Resurrection from the *dead* was certainly a hope clearly taught in the Old Testament. . . .

In the midst of Paul's teaching on the resurrection he says, "Behold, I tell you a mystery; we shall not all sleep, but we shall all be changed" (I Corinthians 15:51).

There are many important truths taught in this verse.

First, Paul says he is introducing a *mystery*. The moment Paul uses the word "mystery," it signals that he is going to reveal a new truth not known before. The word in the original Greek *(mysterion)*, as used in the New Testament, means something not previously known, but now revealed to the true believer.

So what is it that is new? In this chapter he has summed up what was known in the Old Testament: that flesh and blood cannot enter God's presence; that we must first die, then be raised in a new eternal form. The second truth in this verse, and the meaning of the mystery, is that we Christians are not all going *to die!* This was a totally new concept. No Old Testament believer dreamed that some future generation would enter eternity and God's presence without experiencing physical death. Death is an absolute prerequisite to entering immortality through resurrection. . . .

As for the Old Testament believer in general, no one dared to believe that there would be a future generation of believers who would be taken en masse to God's presence.[1]

So there you have it. Christians were told in God's Word that the rapture would indeed take place one day in the future. Although we were not given the exact timing of the event, God gave signs in His Word of what the end times would be like. These signs enabled us to recognize the generation which would see the rapture.

The other question you probably have for us is, "Where did you go?" Well, to put it simply, we went "to heaven to be with the Lord Jesus." Right now, Christians are seeing the fulfillment of Christ's promise when He said, "I go to prepare a place for you. And if I go . . . I will come again and receive you unto myself; that where I am, there ye may be also" (John 14:2,3).

CHAPTER THREE

WHO IS THIS GREAT LEADER?

What does all of this mean? What does the future hold now that Christians are in heaven and you have remained on earth? Does the world just return to normal after this major aberration? These are questions we know must be running through your mind.

Perhaps the most straightforward way to begin is to tell you that the world will never again return to normal. Without stopping to go into the details (we will give you all the details in chapter 9), let us just say that you live in a very unique, very defined time in human history. The Bible calls this time the great tribulation—a seven-year period between the rapture and the second coming of Christ when He will return to this earth to establish His kingdom. We know that this time of tribulation will begin peacefully, but will end with the greatest war in human history.

The Bible also tells us that there will be a central player who will dominate the world stage during this time. Before we go any further, Patti and I want to make sure that you understand that a great leader unlike anyone the world has ever known is about to arise on the world scene. We can only guess, but you probably already know who we are talking about. We believe that he will arise on the scene just moments after we have disappeared.

You need to know in advance that he will be one of the most noble, gentle, wise, and loving persons that the world will have ever encountered. If we were in your world, he would be so convincing that both Patti and I would probably follow after him. But he is the greatest impostor the world has ever known. He is truly a wolf in sheep's clothing. In fact, the Bible tells us that he and other false Christs and false prophets will perform such great miracles that if it were possible, they would deceive even the most faithful followers of God (Matthew 24:24).

This Wolf in Sheep's Clothing

There is no doubt that this leader is the main player in the seven-year drama in which you now find yourself. From his mouth will come extraordinarily subtle, deceptive, and cunning lies. The Bible refers to this person as the Antichrist.

Just to give you an idea of how seriously God takes this leader, he is also addressed in other biblical passages by names such as "the lawless one," "the son of perdition," "the prince of darkness," and "that Wicked." According to our friend Dave Breese, the president of Christian Destiny Inc.:

> The Bible promises that there will arise a figure who ostensibly has the answer to everything. He steps on the scene and in the midst of the present and ever growing disaster he professes to have the answer. You can be very sure that he is going to say "Trust me. Believe in me. Accept my plan. I will be your leader." Who is this person? The Bible teaches that as we move to the consummation of history the Antichrist will appear on the scene. He is so clever. He is so attractive, even so lovable. He will turn out to be the most vicious monster in the form of a ruler that the world has ever seen. This person is the fulfillment of the promise of the rise of Antichrist.[1]

At this point in history, God has not yet revealed the identity of the Antichrist. This has shrouded many discussions with mystery. Back when God had finished unveiling what things would be like in the end times to Daniel, the prophet was confused: "And I heard, but I understood not; then said I, O my Lord, what shall be the end of these things?" God responded, "Go thy way, Daniel, for the words are closed up and sealed till the time of the end" (Daniel 12:8,9). But you now live in that "time of the end," and so we have every reason to believe that, unlike us, you have the ability to identify this Antichrist. We believe that his emergence will coincide closely with the rapture of Christians. In the book of 2 Thessalonians, Paul the apostle explained the rise of this great leader, his relation with the rapture, and the soon return of Jesus Himself to this earth:

> Now we beseech you, brethren, by the coming of our Lord Jesus Christ, and by our gathering together unto him [rapture], that ye be not soon shaken in mind, or be troubled, neither by spirit, nor by word, nor by letter as from us, as that the day of Christ is at hand [second coming]. Let no man deceive you by any means, for that day shall not come, except there come a falling away first, and that man of sin be revealed, the son of perdition. . . . And now ye know what withholdeth that he might be revealed in his time. For the mystery of iniquity doth already work, only he who now letteth will let, until he be taken out of the way. And then shall that Wicked be revealed, whom the Lord shall consume with the spirit of his mouth, and shall destroy with the brightness of his coming (2:1-3,6-8).

What we learn from this passage is very important to our understanding of how things will work in your world. The apostle Paul was talking about the day of Christ—this is the day when Jesus will return to earth (seven biblical years from the day of the rapture). But the apostle, writing under the inspiration of God, foresaw that this could not happen until after the Antichrist was revealed. Furthermore, Paul was shown that the Antichrist, referred to here as the "man of sin," "the son of perdition," and "that Wicked" could not be revealed until something that restrains the Antichrist is taken out of the way. What is that restrainer?

> Some One is preventing the purposes of Satan from coming to culmination and He will keep on performing this ministry until He is removed. . . . It would seem that the only one who could do such a restraining ministry would be the Holy Spirit. . . . As long as the Holy Spirit is resident within the church, which is His temple, this restraining work will continue and the man of sin cannot be revealed. It is only when the church, the temple, is removed that this restraining ministry ceases.[2]

For this reason we believe that the Antichrist will rise onto the world scene very shortly after that which restrains him is removed. With the rapture, this restraint was removed. Thus, the odds are very good that this leader will have already arisen on the world scene in the moment of history that you now find yourself living in.

The more you think about this, the more logical it becomes that this is the most likely time for the rise of this leader from a purely practical point of view. If we can picture your world in the moments and days following the rapture, it is going to be a time of great confusion and chaos. Thoughts, fears, and questions that you and the rest of the world have never pondered are racing through your heads, right? History has taught us that charismatic leaders are not prone to rise on a sea of calm but instead during a time of turmoil and uncertainty. That is when people are looking for a leader. We can't imagine that ever being more true than during the time after the rapture. We know that the Antichrist will give great and soothing explanations for this mass disappearance, and we know that he will promise better times ahead for the people in your world.

But we also know that he will be the greatest deceiver the world has ever known.

The Antichrist Steps onto the World Stage

Today we are witnessing the birth of a global media infrastructure that allows the whole world to see and share in events anywhere on the planet. This is something new for us. We watched it begin to develop years ago with the war between American-led multinational forces and Iraq after it invaded Kuwait. This war was something entirely new because it was the first war that virtually the entire world could watch on live television. It became very addictive and millions of people were glued to their TV sets for days at a time. For the first time we realized the power of new technologies to unite the world through a common experience. It was not just Patti and me watching from Canada, but people all over the world were watching the same images. It gave us a sense of unity, of being a part of the whole planet.

Since that time, there have been other events that have captured the same amount of worldwide attention as television allows us to watch them as they happen. Some of these have taken on a life of their own and have become a major focal point for the entire world's attention.

Why are we telling you this? Because these little examples are only the beginning. They are only a dry run for the way this global media infrastructure will grow by your time. We believe that the greatest media focus in history will have taken place, or is taking place right now, depending on how shortly after the rapture you are reading these words. We believe that much of the world, and probably yourself, has been glued to the TV since this mass disappearance. That makes this media infrastructure a very powerful and very real "player" in the world in which you live. Think about it: TV is probably where most of your information, impressions, interpretations, and explanations are coming from. It has the power to shape your world. Beware of it.

After, or more likely at some point during the coverage of the rapture, we believe the focus of the world's attention will very quickly and very powerfully switch to this new leader. He will ride on the wave of this earth-changing event and will seem to have explanations for what has taken place. He will speak very soothing and comforting words to your ears and will bring a sense of calm and peace to the world and to your heart, unlike anything you have ever known. He will, if we understand the Bible correctly, have a more powerful effect on your mind, soul, and emotions than anything you have ever experienced. Somehow his communication will sweep you up in a wave of oneness, tranquillity, and inner peace.

He is going to speak of the oneness of the human family and of the opportunities for personal and global expansion. He is going to tell, and seemingly show, that you have powers within yourself beyond your wildest dreams. He is going to teach you what love, peace, and joy are all about and he is going to give you experiences that will feel like they are sweeping you into a new level of existence.

The Bible tells us about many of the promises he is going to make and his methods of seduction. By telling you in advance, we hope to prove to you that there is much more going on here than can possibly meet your eye.

Portfolio of This Great Deceiver and His Partner

We have some very strong proof for you from the Bible confirming who this character really is. Probably the greatest condensed source of information on him (and his partner) can be found in the thirteenth chapter of the book of Revelation.

Before we go any further, we want to encourage you to turn to the thirteenth chapter of the book of

Revelation, either in your Bible or in the Appendix at the back of this book. It will help you to get an overall sense of the powers and plans of the one that God calls "the beast" and his partner, who God calls a beast as well. Elsewhere in the book of Revelation God calls this partner "the false prophet."

There are many details and clues given in chapter 13 of the book of Revelation. But for your immediate purposes, we want to highlight a few of the key facts about this great deceiver so that you can be certain he is indeed the one the Bible is warning you about.

Clue #1: A head wound that seems to be miraculously healed. One of the first things this chapter tells us about is a seemingly fatal head wound that this leader will appear to miraculously recover from. The Bible uses symbolism to give us clues about this beast. It is not a literal creature with seven heads and ten horns. This symbolism is developed throughout the passages of the Bible to give us some background on this newly emerging world leader. However, we believe the third verse of chapter 13 refers to a literal event that may well catapult him to world prominence and to actually becoming the object of worship by the people of the world.

From where we sit, this is something hard to imagine, and we don't understand exactly how it will happen. But the third and fourth verses of Revelation 13 indicate that something unlike anything in world history will take place in your time:

> And I saw one of his heads as it were
> wounded to death; and his deadly wound

> was healed, and all the world wondered
> after the beast. And they worshipped the
> dragon which gave power unto the beast,
> and they worshipped the beast.

This clue is mentioned because it may well be one of the first things that takes place after the rapture. We can't be sure of this, but since it is referred to so early in this chapter it may imply a chronology of events. One thing is definite, it is going to happen at some point. And when this "miraculous" healing occurs, it is going to be an earth-shattering event.

This miraculous event will cut through every culture, race, belief, and religion and unite the world in a single worldwide faith. Through this event, the Antichrist will get virtually every person on the face of the earth—even the most devout beer-swilling atheists—to actually fall down and worship him.

And if we can understand it from our perspective on this side of the rapture, it will be a faith centered around the worship of this man and of what he claims gave him the power to be healed. In these verses the Bible claims that the source of this great power is Satan himself, symbolized by the dragon.

There won't appear to be anything evil about this event. It will seem to be one of the most touching, humane, and miraculous events the world has ever witnessed. In fact, though we are getting ahead of ourselves here, we believe that this deceiver, while accepting the world's worship, may say something to the effect of, "Yes, I'm a god and worthy of worship, but you too can become a god just like me.

You can share in these great powers. Let me show you the way."

Clue #2: His first words will be an attack against God. The thirteenth chapter of Revelation is very clear about the first words that will come from this deceiver's mouth. Please don't overlook how significant a clue this is, especially given the fact that it was foretold almost 2000 years ago!

Under the inspiration of the Holy Spirit, the apostle John saw that this leader would have one of the most charismatic voices the world has ever known and that the first words out of his mouth— his central message, his core theme—would be an instantaneous and focused attack on God Himself.

We'll talk about this more later, but we want to remind you that this attack on God is one of the most important clues to the fact that this leader, his activities, and even his words have been long foretold by the very God who is allowing him this horrible, deceptive moment on planet earth.

Clue #3: He is going to make war on those who now accept Jesus as their Savior. Revelation 13 makes it clear that not only is this Antichrist going to speak horrible and blasphemous words against the Lord, but he is also going to actively track down and persecute those who believe that Jesus is the Messiah.

In Revelation 13:7 we read, "It was given unto him to make war with the saints, and to overcome them." But this is far from the only reference to the all-out war the Antichrist is going to wage against those who become believers in the true Christ. We will talk more about this later, but make sure that you keep this clue on your list so that you can confirm to yourself who this impostor really is. Through the veneer of love for all people, he will have a true hatred for those who trust Jesus. That will be the big sin of your time.

Clue #4: He is going to finally unite the world in a seemingly great new world order. Revelation 13 tells us that your world will witness the coming together of three key components that will make up a new world order. We have already mentioned the emergence of a worldwide religion. Verse 8 says specifically that *"all* that dwell upon the earth shall worship him."* The word *all* is important because the apostle John is stressing throughout the entire chapter the global spread of not only a religious system, but also of the other two components of the new world order.

Verse 7 indicates that this beast will control the entire globe politically as well as religiously. Here we read that "power was given him over *all* kindreds, and tongues, and nations." In our time the idea of a new world order with a global political authority is just beginning to come to the fore. Never before in history has there been a single world government. But according to the Bible, you will see it in your time.

Finally, verses 16-18 tell us of the third component of the new world order. This is the all-important economic portion. Once again John is clear: The new economic system, built around every person receiving a mark in his right hand or forehead, will be imposed on *all.*

We foresee this beast proposing and leading a world government, a world religion, and a global economy. The Bible in Ecclesiastes 4:12 says a three-fold cord is not easily broken, and it is clear that this threefold new world order will not easily be broken either. But make no mistake about it: It will be broken by Jesus when He returns.

What Is the New World Order, and Who Is This Guy?

Let's look at a bit of background on this new world order. We think this will give you a bit of insight into the great leader and his true goals. So far we've told you how to recognize him and some of the things he will do, but we have not fully told you who he is and what this is all about.

The events that are occurring in your world are far from random political, economic, and religious developments. In fact, each and every one of these events and developments has a significant meaning. If you can understand some of them, you will be able to understand why God is allowing all of this to happen and why this enemy of God is trying to lead you down his path.

Even if you have had little exposure to the Bible before now, you have probably heard of the kingdom of God. If you recall the Lord's prayer, it begins with "Our Father, who art in heaven. Hallowed be thy name. Thy kingdom come." Throughout the Bible, God promised that one day His kingdom would indeed come. That promise will begin to find its real and true fulfillment when Jesus returns to this earth at the end of the seven-year period in which you are now living. After that time, He will establish His kingdom here on earth for 1000 years. It will be a time when mankind will finally see the world the way God intended it to be.

This plan would have come into action thousands of years ago had Eve not eaten the forbidden fruit in the Garden of Eden. She was deceived into thinking that she knew better than God. However, Eve was only the first of an entire race to repeat the same mistake. And what Eve did on a personal level, mankind has also done time and time again on a global level. Man has always thought he could build a world of peace and harmony (like the one in the Garden of Eden or in the coming 1000-year kingdom) without God.

The first example of this was something called the Tower of Babel. This tower, which is spoken of in the book of Genesis, was much more than a physical tower. It was actually a ziggurat, or a structure, to map the stars for the purposes of astrology. It was man's attempt to "come together as one," to build a society that could reach heavenly proportions without the help of God. God saw what was happening, and so to protect mankind from mass deception, He confused their language so that no one could understand each other. This is where the word *babble* comes from.

In our day there is an emerging force in Europe called the European Union. We believe it will become the heart of the global empire in the future.

One of its leaders is a man by the name of Helmut
Kohl, who is the Chancellor of Germany. Here is
how he sees the future:

> The United States of Europe will form
> the core of a peaceful order . . . the age
> prophesied of old, when all shall dwell
> secure and none shall make them afraid.[3]

It is frightening when mankind thinks of doing
what God has said only He can do. If it were an iso-
lated statement or idea, that would be one thing.
But what Patti and I want you to understand is that
this whole idea is beginning to dominate the planning and thinking of our world in the same way it
will dominate yours.

The United Nations is another perfect example.
We don't know exactly what role the United
Nations will play in the future. We don't know if it
will be strengthened and fully functional, or if it
will simply be the philosophical precursor to the
empire that is beginning to rule your world. But we
do know the idea that will underlie this empire:
Man can build his own kingdom. This is the central
thinking of the United Nations. You can't get much
more to the heart of an organization than the words
chiseled into the cornerstone of its headquarters,
right? Well, here's what the United Nations has
etched into the foundation stone of its building:

> And they shall beat their swords into
> plowshares, and their spears into pruning-
> hooks: nation shall not lift up sword

against nation, neither shall they learn war
anymore.

Well, there are several very interesting things
about this United Nations motto. First, it actually
comes from the Bible. It is a promise lifted from the
book of Isaiah, the second chapter, which is speaking about the millennial kingdom with Jesus ruling
the earth. Yet, the United Nations has not only left
the clear references to the Lord out, but it has also
taken His role upon itself!

But the Lord knew that this would happen. For
this reason He had another one of His prophets warn
about this attempt to build the kingdom of peace
without the Prince of Peace. Man's prideful attempts
to build his own kingdom will lead to the exact
opposite of what will happen when Jesus returns:

> Proclaim ye this among the Gentiles;
> Prepare war, wake up the mighty men, let
> all the men of war draw near; let them
> come up. Beat your plowshares into
> swords, and your pruninghooks into
> spears (Joel 3:9,10).

The Same Vision at the Heart of Communism

Communism is widely accepted as the most evil
form of government in the world's history. But the
Communists believe that utopian ends justify cruel
and harsh means. According to a well-respected his-
torian:

The one poetic touch in Lenin's otherwise abrasive mind, in fact, concerned the almost dreamlike "Worker's Paradise" he saw at the end of the proletarian rainbow. To find a parallel, you would have to go back to the early Hebrew prophets and their forecast of the Messianic Age . . . men and women, workers all, living in a stateless society under conditions of endless plenty, absolute justice and perpetual peace among nations.[4]

We Say All That to Say This

The most deadly of the deadly sins is pride. Thus it should come as no surprise that mankind has always striven to build his own kingdom without the help of God. Indeed, this great leader not only wants to lead you in building your own kingdom, but he also wants to try to get you to join him in proclaiming that you are God.

What we want you to understand is that this new world order that the Antichrist is leading the world into is directly opposed to God. God promised that He would establish His kingdom on earth with Jesus ruling over it while sitting on the throne of David in Jerusalem.

In the original Greek language, the "anti" in *Antichrist* has the connotation of not only being against but also of being "in place of, an impostor." So it should come as no surprise that Satan, the master of counterfeiters, should seek to replace God's kingdom with this new world order and replace

Jesus Christ with the Antichrist. The Antichrist may even claim that he is the latest incarnation of the "Christ Spirit," coming back to lead the world into true spiritual enlightenment. This is a game plan that was hatched in the heavens, introduced in the Garden of Eden, perfected at the ancient Tower of Babel and the modern United Nations, and is now swinging into full motion. Satan knows the Scriptures. And he knows his time is short. Now is his last chance to deceive the world into worshiping him instead of God.

So Why Is God Allowing This?

No doubt you are perplexed by the life-changing events you are witnessing and experiencing. Perhaps you are confused by these words that you are reading, and the question that has come to your mind is, "Why is God allowing this?"

Please understand that at the end of the seven-year period in which you are living, God is going to judge mankind. And a part of that judgment will have to do with man's pride and his conviction that he does not need the help or grace of God. This is a very important point because if mankind could have built a kingdom of peace without God, then God's plan of salvation and faith would be unnecessary.

But if the Lord were to judge the earth right now in my day, mankind could answer back and say, "Hey, wait a minute! We were just about to get it all together before You came back here and interrupted everything!" This is why God is allowing this time of trouble that you are now living through.

Remember that this world leader isn't forcing anyone to follow him. Virtually everyone on the planet has listened to his words, to his tirade against God, and they are not only agreeing with him, they are worshiping him. They also believe that man can build his own kingdom. God is giving them free rein to try. At other times in history God intervened before things got too out-of-hand. He did so with the flood in Noah's day and again at the Tower of Babel. But this time He will not intervene. He has to let mankind try so that it will see the result of this millennia-old effort.

We have a theory. We know from the Bible that the seven-year period you are now living in ends with the Battle of Armageddon. This will be the greatest battle in human history. In fact, Jesus makes a very interesting statement about this time in history. He says,

> For then shall be great tribulation, such as was not since the beginning of the world to this time, no, nor ever shall be. And except those days should be shortened, there should no flesh be saved, but for the elect's sake those days shall be shortened (Matthew 24:21-22).

Based on this, we wonder if the possibility exists that the various armies will have launched a nuclear strike and counterstrike at the height of the Battle of Armageddon. The nuclear warheads would all be in the air, and this might be the moment when Jesus returns. At that moment, mankind could not give the excuse, "Hey, we were just about to get it all together!"

CHAPTER FOUR

THE FALSE PROPHET

During the tribulation the Antichrist does not act alone. He has a partner, who, according to the Bible, is called the false prophet. In fact, there will be three principal evil personalities in that time—a kind of unholy trilogy.

Lucifer or Satan was an angel in heaven in the very early days of history. But he wanted to be God. And because of his pride and resulting rebellion, God kicked him out of heaven. Ever since then, Satan has been trying to deceive and lead mankind away from the true God. Satan, not being God, has only been able to imitate and copy things of God.

And one of his imitations is the trilogy. God's holy Trinity is made up of God the Father, His Son Jesus Christ, and the Holy Spirit who draws men to Jesus.

Satan's version of the trilogy is made up first of himself, also known in the Bible as the dragon. Then there is the Antichrist whom we talked about in the last chapter, also known as the beast. And finally there is the false prophet, who is the main focus of this chapter.

These three characters are referred to all together in Revelation 16:13: the dragon, the beast, and the false prophet. The dragon imitates God. The beast is an impostor of Jesus Christ. And the false prophet imitates the role of the Holy Spirit, drawing men to the Antichrist.

Signs and Wonders

About 2000 years ago when Jesus Christ was on earth, He performed many miracles. He turned water into wine at a wedding feast. He raised Lazarus from the dead. He healed the lame and blind and cast out demons. He performed these miracles through the power of the Holy Spirit.

The Holy Spirit enabled the disciples of Jesus to perform miracles, especially after Jesus had ascended to heaven. They were able to heal the lame and the blind. The apostle Paul restored life to a young man who died from a fall during one of Paul's sermons (the guy fell asleep and fell off a rafter!). These are only a few examples. There were many miracles in the early days of the church. We believe that God is always the same, and what was possible then is possible now. Miracles are just not as frequent. For most of the church age, we saw very few *true* miracles like those experienced by the early church. We lived in an age of grace whereby we were to believe in God and His Son, Jesus Christ, by faith. In 2 Corinthians 4:18 we are told:

> While we look not at the things which are seen, but at the things which are not seen, for the things which are seen are temporal; but the things which are not seen are eternal.

And in Hebrews 11, verses 1 and 6, we are told:

> Now faith is the substance of things hoped for, the evidence of things not seen. But without faith it is impossible to please him, for he that cometh to God must believe that he is, and that he is a rewarder of them that diligently seek him.

However, in the last days leading up to the rapture of believers in Jesus, there has been a growing interest in signs and wonders, both among believers and non-Christians. Many have begun to see the ability to perform signs and wonders as proof of the validity of their beliefs. The problem is that many people with varying beliefs, often directly opposed to each other, seem to be able to manifest these signs or wonders.

The fact is that many of these seeming miracles are fraudulent, based more on sleight of hand than

on any spiritual powers. But there are many instances in which much more than a magician's trade
is being plied. We believe that this is happening
because we are indeed drawing closer to the time in
which you live, with only the rapture separating us.

Signs and Wonders Will Be the Order of Your Day

There is little doubt that signs, wonders, and miracles will be at the heart of the world in which you
live. Looking through this prism in time, Patti and I
believe that every notion, every idea, and every theory of reality will be challenged and questioned.
People will seem to have newfound powers, and
things thought impossible in our world will become
commonplace in yours.

The Bible is very specific about this. So before we
talk about the false prophet, let us remind you that
these seemingly miraculous things you are witnessing were foretold by God a long time ago and may
not be what they seem:

> Even him [the Antichrist], whose com-
> ing is after the working of Satan *with all
> power and signs and lying wonders,* and with
> all deceivableness . . . (2 Thessalonians
> 2:9,10).

> For there shall arise false Christs, and
> false prophets, and shall show great signs
> and wonders; insomuch that, if it were
> possible, they shall deceive the very elect
> (Matthew 24:24).

Indeed, during your time in the tribulation there will be great emphasis on signs and wonders. But nowhere will these signs be as powerful as in the hands of the false prophet.

Clue #1: The false prophet will be able to make fire fall from heaven. As we've just read, 2 Thessalonians 2:9 tells us that the Antichrist himself will be able to perform great signs and wonders. But signs and wonders are really going to be the specialty of the false prophet. For example, he will *literally* be able to call fire down from heaven in the sight of the Antichrist and an onlooking multitude. This is something very specific that you can watch for.

You can read about this false prophet in Revelation chapter 13, verses 11-14:

> And I beheld another beast [the false prophet] coming up out of the earth; and he had two horns like a lamb, and he spoke as a dragon. And he exerciseth all of the power of the first beast [the Antichrist] before him, and causeth the earth and them which dwell therein to worship the first beast, whose deadly wound was healed. And he doeth great wonders, so that he maketh fire come down from heaven on the earth in the sight of men, and deceiveth them that dwell on the earth by the means of those miracles which he had power to do in the sight of the beast.

By his powers the false prophet will be able to deceive people on earth, causing them to worship the beast, or the Antichrist. Satan knows that it is difficult for people to believe by faith as God requires. So he deceives people with signs and wonders into following him and his minions—the Antichrist and the false prophet.

Clue #2: The false prophet will make an image that lives and speaks. We are daily watching technological marvels coming into existence that boggle the mind. Science fiction takes our imaginations even a step further. "Star Trek" is probably the most popular science-fiction program of them all. The weekly voyages of Captain Kirk and Jean-Luc Picard, played and replayed, ignite the imaginations of this generation. One specific item of Trek lore that we want to mention here is something called the holodeck.

The holodeck is a fictional room in which the crew of the *Enterprise* can live out their fantasies. Once the room is programmed by computer, a crew member is surrounded in a virtual world of his own creation. Scenes, sites, and characters all come to life around him and engulf him in this virtual reality. However, the whole world is made up of holograms which are nothing more than images of light. With the words "Computer, end program," the whole virtual world simply vanishes. The interesting question for our world is, "How much of this is fiction and how much is fact?" There are some people who believe that the scientific capability exists to make virtual reality possible, but we are just waiting for computers fast enough to do the billions of instantaneous calculations necessary. After all, we do live in a time when mannequins in some department stores are already being replaced with holographic models made up of nothing but light.

Whether this technology will be involved or not, we cannot be certain. But the Bible indicates that the greatest image the world has ever seen will be brought to life by the hands of the false prophet:

> And [he] deceiveth them that dwell on the earth by the means of those miracles which he had power to do in the sight of the beast; saying to them that dwell on earth, that they should make an image to the beast, which had the wound by a sword, and did live. And he had power to give life unto the image of the beast, that the image of the beast should both speak, and cause that as many as would not worship the image of the beast should be killed (Revelation 13:14,15).

We have no idea exactly how this will come about, but once again, the Bible is very specific that it will happen. Keep watching, and let the fact that God has told you ahead of time help build your faith and lead you to make the right but very difficult decision when the time comes. One of the most beautiful promises in the Bible is that if we trust Him, God will always give us strength equal to the challenge. Don't forget that as powerful as Satan and his minions seem to be, they are only cheap counterfeits of the real Miracle Worker!

Clue #3: The false prophet will try to make you receive a mark in your hand or forehead. We'll talk more about this in an upcoming chapter, but Revelation 13 also gives us another insight into the character and activities of this false prophet. This deceiver will establish a system whereby everyone on earth will have to receive a mark in his right hand or forehead in order to be able to buy or sell anything:

> And he causeth all, both small and great, rich and poor, free and bond, to receive a mark in their right hand, or in their foreheads, and that no man might buy or sell, save he that had the mark, or the name of the beast, or the number of his name (Revelation 13:16,17).

Please don't ever take this mark. We'll tell you all about it in chapter 6, but taking it will be the worst mistake made since Eve ate the forbidden fruit in the Garden of Eden. Remember how specific the Bible has been in foretelling all this. Let that build and encourage your faith.

Why Shouldn't I Believe Them?

Just because someone can perform a sign or a wonder doesn't mean he is telling the truth, does it? Of course not. That is why God always gave much more than a few signs and wonders by which to know Him. He gave us an entire book through which we could come to know and understand Him. As we walk with Him, He leads and teaches us His ways. And He will do the same for you today, right now, in the world in which you live.

One of the things you need to remember, however, is this: Don't believe everything you see. Miracles, powers, and noble words cannot be trusted:

> For such are false apostles, deceitful workers, transforming themselves into the apostles of Christ. And no marvel; for Satan himself is transformed into an angel of light (2 Corinthians 11:13-14).

Many years ago the Israelites were slaves in Egypt. God sent Moses as His messenger to Egypt, telling Pharaoh to let the Israelites go. Moses was able to perform signs and wonders in front of Pharaoh and his court to prove that God was real and that He wanted Pharaoh to let His people go.

Pharaoh refused. His magicians tried to prove that Moses had no more power than they did. Up to a point, they were able to duplicate the signs and wonders that Moses did. But only up to a point. When Moses' rod was turned into a serpent, so were the rods of the magicians. But Moses' serpent then ate theirs.

What we are trying to say is that God told you this was going to happen. He told you how power-ful these signs would be. But He is also offering you proof that He is God by foretelling all this. This is something that only He can truly do. As you will see, He will also show you clearly who is behind all these signs and wonders. If you want to be led, He will lead you. All you have to do is believe and follow Him.

CHAPTER FIVE

WHAT ARE SOME OF THE EXCUSES YOU WILL HEAR FOR THE VANISHING?

Let's take a moment and go back to the question that must still be swirling around in your mind. Who left and where did they go? Patti and I already showed you the explanation the Bible has given for this great vanishing thousands of years before it happened. Also explained were the reasons why we were able to understand what was about to take place when we wrote these words to you.

In addition, we know that the greatest leader the world has ever seen is probably already on the scene. There is little doubt that he will have great and soothing explanations for what has happened.

Plus we know that the explanations will be so compelling that every aspect of your being will want to believe that the story is true. But don't forget that if this guy is really who the Bible says he is, he knows what buttons to push in people's hearts and minds. He has been in the business of deception for a long, long time.

The Same Old Reminder

Patti and I have a great fear as we write these words to you. We are worried because, while we do understand many of the events that will take place in your time, there are other areas where we have to speculate a little. In most instances, we feel we have a general sense of what will happen. But the fact is that we are looking through a prism in time and into a world we cannot possibly comprehend.

And therein lies our fear. In our attempt to show you the detail the Bible does give, we may misunderstand some of the clues given. What we ask you to do is take the clues that the Bible gives and keep those separate from our interpretation of them. We are fallible; the Bible is not. We guess this is our way of saying that where we do not understand perfectly, don't throw the baby out with the bathwater.

Nothing Is What It Seems

If there is one word that can best describe the time in which you are now living, it is *deception!*

As we shared earlier, when Jesus was asked what it would be like before His return to this earth, the very first words He uttered were a warning against deception. And now that the rapture has taken place and the restraining influence of the Holy Spirit has been removed, we believe that you are in the heart of this period of unparalleled deception. This deception, we believe, will also include a diabolically clever lie regarding what has happened to those who have vanished and why you are still here.

Who Left?

There should be little dispute about who has left. It seems likely that it will quickly become clear that all those who are gone had something in common. Whether they lived in Canada, China, Russia, or anywhere else in the world, those of us who left all shared one thing: We believed that Jesus was the Son of God, and we had accepted Him as Lord.

That does not mean that everyone who said he or she was a Christian has vanished. And this fact will greatly confuse the issue. Many preachers, priests, and members of churches will still be living in your world. Of course, they will argue against anyone saying that it is "Christians who have vanished." They will almost certainly argue that it is the false Christians, the misfits, who have disappeared.

However, if the Bible is true, don't forget that by definition these men, no matter how high a church position they hold, were not true Christians when the rapture took place, or they too would have vanished. Beware of them. We believe that they will be among the most deceptive and dangerous supporters of the

Antichrist and his false prophet. Having been so close to the light, they will now be consumed by the darkness.

What we are saying is that it will generally be accepted that those who vanished shared a common faith. But it will probably also be widely perceived that they were those who were misfits in some way. This is where the deception will start to get really interesting—in response to the question "Where did they go?"

The Bible does not tell us what the Antichrist's theory will be. In fact, the Bible does not give us a detailed explanation for this event at all. This means that we have to do a bit of speculation. But before we do that, let's address one of the things that we do know.

The Explanation Will Seem to Prove "The Lie"

The purpose of the new world order is to get everyone to believe a very specific lie. When we earlier mentioned the new world order, we explained part of the lie to you. The basic thrust of this movement is to get you to believe that you don't need God to come and rescue the world, that you have the power to do that yourself. You certainly don't need some outmoded promise of "a new heaven and new earth." The new age of peace and prosperity can be built here on this earth.

But there is a more basic, a more fundamental lie that underlies this one. It is behind the whole history of this world and of Satan's conflict with God before this world was even created. Let us go back and explore that story. It is amazing how central it is to the world in which you live and the climax of history that is just a few short years away.

There was a time in heaven when an angel named Lucifer was the highest of all angels in God's domain. Yet one day he conceived a lie in his heart, a lie telling him that he could be greater than his Creator. On that day God cast him out of heaven:

> How art thou fallen from heaven, O Lucifer, son of the morning! How art thou cut down to the ground which didst weaken the nations! For thou hast said in thine heart, *I will* ascend into heaven, *I will* exalt my throne above the stars of God: *I will* sit also upon the mount of the congregation, in the sides of the north. *I will* ascend above the heights of the clouds; *I will be like the most High* (Isaiah 14:12-14, emphasis added).

Having seduced himself with this lie that he had created, Lucifer was cast from heaven and became the temporary ruler of this earth. You may recall that Lucifer used this exact same lie to deceive Eve in the Garden of Eden.

God told Adam and Eve that they could eat of any tree in the garden except one—the tree of the knowledge of good and evil. God said that if they ate the fruit from this tree they would die spiritually. But Lucifer, the serpent, knowing the power of the lie, subtly seduced Eve with that same lie:

> And the serpent said unto the woman, Ye shall not surely die, for God doth know

that in the day ye eat thereof, then your eyes shall be opened, *and ye shall be as gods* (Genesis 3:4,5, emphasis added).

In the thousands of years that have transpired since that fateful day, Satan's lie has not changed. The promise that if man will throw off the shackles of faith in God, he will discover that he is truly a god himself has been Satan's modus operandi throughout all of history. In fact, this has been the core teaching of virtually every false religion and cult. Let us give you just a few examples of how widely this lie has been spread through Satan's impostor religions:

The devil told the truth [about godhood] . . . I do not blame Mother Eve. I would not have had her miss eating the forbidden fruit for anything.

—Brigham Young, former president, Mormon Church[1]

The absolute assumption that a lot of us are making in the Holistic Health Movement is that all of the things necessary to create my life are in me. . . . I believe that I am God, and I believe that you are.

—Jack Gibbs, psychologist[2]

You are a god in your universe.

—Werner Erhard, founder of est[3]

Man is an emerging God. . . . My plan and my duty is to reveal to you a new way . . . which will permit the divine in man to shine forth.
—Benjamin Creme, New Age leader[4]

Be still and know that you are God.
—Maharishi Mahesh Yogi, founder of Transcendental Meditation[5]

God and man are one. Man is an incarnate God.
—Sun Myung Moon, founder of the Unification Church[6]

The Core of Any Explanation

As we have said before, we are uncertain of exactly how the Antichrist will explain the rapture to you. However, we can be very confident that whatever explanation he gives, it will promote this core lie that you can be a god. He wants you to believe that you are your own god! He wants you to believe that you have powers within yourself, and that if you will just let him help you tap into these powers, you will discover a reality unlike anything you have ever imagined.

It will seem convincing. He will offer startling proofs for his promises, but it is the oldest and most successful lie ever used for deceiving human hearts. And you are seeing it in its most potent form.

With these facts in mind, let's look at some of our speculations as to which components may well be part of the Antichrist's explanation for what is going on in your world.

Another Old Lie: Evolution

One of the most persistent theories concerning the origin of man, if God didn't create us, has been evolution. Over the past decades this theory has remarkably come to be considered legitimate science despite the fact that more and more research is discrediting it as even being a viable theory.

How does this old debate tie into your world? The evolution debate in our time before the rapture has taken on an intriguing twist. The discussion among many evolutionists is not just about how mankind came into existence in some mud puddle millions of years ago. Many argue that since evolution is an ongoing process, not just something that happened eons ago, then we can expect mankind to evolve even further.

Interestingly, because they cannot find the missing links in their evolutionary chains, many scientists who are unwilling to discard their theories have suggested that maybe evolution does not happen slowly over millions of years after all. Maybe it happens very suddenly in what they call quantum leaps. Putting these two ideas together, many people believe that mankind is about to experience another sudden leap in the evolutionary process.

But there is another twist to this new science. Until recently, evolution has been thought of in physical terms. But in these last days before the rapture, many evolutionists are beginning to suggest that this next quantum leap will be spiritual, not physical. They argue that increased instances of psychic powers, telepathy, and other mental powers in some members of the population foreshadow a coming evolution for the entire species.

Willis Harman, a former consultant to the National Goals Research Staff of the White House and a professor at Stanford Research Institute (SRI), put it this way:

> Psychic phenomena are anomalous— their occurrence is widely attested to, yet they do not conform to known physical and biological laws. They do suggest however, that something is fundamentally incomplete about a world view which cannot accommodate their existence. . . . The types of papers currently being presented at scientific meetings and articles being published in the most prestigious scientific journals suggest that, with regard to both consciousness research, and psychic research, the transition from rejection to acceptance may be at hand.[7]

One day soon, they believe, mankind as a whole will discover how to use the godlike inner potential that supposedly lies within us all. As one New Ager put it, "If men and women have ultimately come up from amoebas, then they are all ultimately on their way towards God."[8]

Part of a Mass Evolutionary Leap?

One proponent of spiritual evolution in our time is Barbara Marx Hubbard. She was a Democratic party nominee for the position of vice president at the Democratic National Convention in 1984. She sees this as an event of biblical proportions and says such a quantum leap would bring about

> . . . a mass transfiguration and empow-
> erment of millions at once . . . a second
> coming through lifting our consciousness,
> transforming ourselves as Christ trans-
> formed himself. . . . Such events are now
> being prepared.[9]

While such ideas are not widely accepted in our world today, many reputable scientists are beginning to look into these things. And as silly as they may seem today, we think your world may eagerly accept these ideas.

Why? Because you will be living in a unique and extraordinary time. Things that don't happen in our world will happen in yours. It will be a time of miracles and signs and wonders. In such a new reality it makes sense that people will be seeking new answers.

As we have said, the Bible says that these signs and wonders are the work of seducing spirits who are now no longer restrained by the Holy Spirit. But the world is by and large not going to accept this explanation. Yours is a time when the Bible will be hated and not referred to as a source of information for what is taking place. Thus we can understand that other explanations for these phenomena will be offered, just as different explanations will be provided for the rapture. And this idea of a quantum leap and spiritual evolution fits in with the lies that the devil is now trying to foist on you through his anointed leader and the false prophet.

Remember, the idea of evolution is itself in direct opposition to God's creation of the world and of mankind. If you can be persuaded to believe in evolution, then everything in the world changes, especially in light of the seeming proof for the quantum leap you are being told has just happened. For the first time in history you may be witnessing the development of a new worldwide faith built on the ultimate humanism.

If mankind is evolving, and if that evolution is spiritual, doesn't it seem to prove the central lie of Lucifer in the Garden of Eden? After all, if you keep evolving into higher and higher spiritual forms, there would seem to come a time when "you shall be as gods."

It's the Scam of the Century (and Beyond)

There is an amazing (but not surprising) correlation between Satan's oldest lie and the idea of spiritual evolution. And the clever trap that is being set by the one that God calls "the father of lies" is so powerful, so subtle, and so compelling that we are convinced that almost everyone on earth in your time will be pulled into it.

Part of the power of this lie comes from the fact that it plays right into mankind's weakest point: pride. There is nothing quite so liberating to the human mind as the idea that man has no one to answer to and that all power lies within himself. Equally compelling is the idea that these lofty proclamations seem to be based on science, not religion. Think about that for a second. Science is based on observation and analysis. In your world scientists will indeed be able to observe some very real and very distinct phenomena taking place. We're talking about miracles and signs and wonders. How can they explain these new powers that people have? Won't it seem that people have tapped into a new realm of mental powers?

But wait a minute. Science is based on observing all the facts and coming to a conclusion based on those facts. However, the Bible tells us that in your world the cause of these events will be undetected by even the very brightest scientists. Indeed, the very demons that science denies exist will be pulling the strings behind the scenes to deceive the world into believing the lie. What a field day Satan and his minions will have in using science, man's loftiest boast of pride and achievement, as a tool to enslave him.

Years ago the Bible warned us to beware of the "oppositions of science falsely so called" (1 Timothy 6:20). Never has this been more true. Remember, the rule of thumb in your day is that nothing will be as it appears.

If Mankind Just Evolved, What Happened to Those Who Left?

Evolution represents a time of great change. The same people in our time who preach the coming change also preach that those who cannot make the change stand in the way of its fulfillment.

Thus, it is not surprising that proponents of the spiritual evolution philosophy also teach that those who stand in the way of evolutionary progress will have to be removed. So as we said earlier, you may indeed hear that it *was* some of the Christians who experienced a mass disappearance. But you will be told that it was not because we were believers in Jesus Christ, but because we were bad people. We were the people who were afraid of change and tried to stop it. Here's how one writer sees the issue:

> Religious fundamentalists are convinced that we are living in the end times and that this era will end in nuclear holocaust. The fundamentalists believe those who are born again will be removed by God to meet Jesus in the air through what they call the rapture before the great tribulation that will destroy the earth. . . . There is a force in history that unites Humanity, but the fundamentalists do not share this vision.[10]

As students of Bible prophecy on this side of the rapture, we are amazed to see the growing hatred toward biblical Christians foreshadowing the out-right persecution that will exist in your day. However, it is even more fascinating to see the devil and his minions laying the groundwork for false explanations of what this great disappearance really was. Barbara Marx Hubbard says that her spirit guides (demons) explained it this way:

Humanity will not be able to make the transition for Earth-only to universal life until the chaff has been separated from the wheat. The great reaper must reap before we can take the quantum-leap to the next phase of evolution. . . . This act is as horrible as killing a cancer cell. It must be done for the sake of the future of the whole. . . . We have no choice, dearly beloveds. It is a case of the destruction of the whole planet, or the elimination of the ego-driven, godless one-fourth who, at this time of planetary birth, can, if allowed to live on to reproduce their defective disconnection, destroy forever the opportunity of homo sapiens to become homo universalis.[11]

New Age leader Ruth Montgomery's spirit guides are even more to the point. She says they have told her that:

Those who survive the shift will be a different type of people. . . . The souls who helped to bring on the chaos of the present century will *have passed into the spirit to rethink their attitudes. . . . Millions will survive and millions won't. Those that won't will go into the spirit state.*[12]

New Powers for Those Left Behind

There's another reason why the less enlightened must be removed according to New Agers. At the

Democratic National Convention in 1984, Hubbard showed that the spirit guides who were communicating with her understood that they would indeed be able to give people deceptive powers after the rapture. This is another reason, according to Hubbard and her guides, that some must be removed from earth:

> Christ-consciousness and Christ abilities are the natural inheritance of every human being now on Earth. . . . All who choose to be natural Christs will be guided from within as to how to proceed. All who choose not to evolve will die off; their souls will begin again within a different planetary system which will serve as kindergarten for the transition from self-centered to whole-centered beings. . . . To allow self-centered humans to enter the next stage of evolution would be like giving a two-year-old child the powers of a psychic surgeon, a genetic engineer, and a Chief of Staff of the nuclear forces of the world!
>
> Just as any cell, once cancerous, can infect the whole body with destructive growth, every human in the body of humanity can destroy the whole after a certain stage of power has been collectively attained. . . .
>
> In such circumstances, only the good can evolve. Since the powers of co-creation are also powers of co-destruction, there is a built-in limit to selfishness just as there is with the cancerous cell. If either succeeds, it surely fails, killing the whole system that sustains it. If one

person in a state of selfishness were to inherit the powers of a natural Christ, he could destroy the universe. This cannot be.[13]

While this is, of course, not a full explanation for such New Age beliefs, it does go to show that the idea of an evolving mankind and the disappearance of those who stand in the way is very much at the heart of the metaphysical world of our day.

However, a very interesting question still remains. Where will it be said that those who disappeared went? We're back to the second half of our very first question: "Who left and where did they go?"

You may have an idea of a possible deceptive answer from the quotes above. Ruth Montgomery said above, "The souls who helped to bring on the chaos of the present century will have passed into the spirit to rethink their attitudes. . . . [They] will go into the spirit state." Hubbard said above that "their souls will begin again within a different planetary system which will serve as kindergarten for the transition from self-centered to whole-centered beings."

And, indeed, these ideas *are* very much at the heart of esoteric thinking today. There is the idea that backward people who were unwilling to grow and evolve will be transported into another dimension or onto other planets for a sort of remedial learning program. It almost sounds like science fiction.

New Answers for a New Generation

In the late twentieth century we live in a time of exciting and fascinating scientific advances. Things are happening so quickly that almost anything seems possible—if not today, then tomorrow or the next day.

For the first time in history we have become conditioned to expect and anticipate change. It seems that the only thing that remains constant is change. And the change is happening so quickly that we are often confused between what has been invented and what we saw on "Star Trek" last week. It truly is an exciting and often bewildering time.

In this world where science has often been confused with science fiction, we are given completely different answers to our questions. Is the world truly headed for judgment and destruction? "No" say those at the helm of the good ship *Enterprise.* They say we are just beginning to explore the universe and ourselves and to join the United Federation of Planets.

Were we created by God? "No. A thousand times no! Don't you understand that we were planted here by aliens millions of years ago? Don't you know that they have watched over us and only return now because we are facing self-destruction at the same time that we have reached a level where we are ready to join the universal civilization?"

So is there a God? "Of course not, my child. Things that seemed miraculous and mysterious to you were just technologies you didn't understand. Men like Jesus, Buddha, and Mohammed were just astronauts we tried to send to you to help you see that you could develop the same powers they had. But you misunderstood and worshiped them without realizing that they wanted you to worship yourself as well."

So these people who vanished were not caught up to meet the Lord in the air and to be with Him forever? "Goodness no, my little one! Surely you have seen the transporter beam on your TV show 'Star Trek.' We have just 'beamed these people up' because they are not ready for the next step."

Beam Me Up, Scotty

Think about it for a second. What is the one image that everyone in the world has for seeing someone vanish in front of their eyes? You've got it. It's the transporter beam on "Star Trek." That makes us wonder if that might be a part of the explanation of this mass disappearance. And as we've pondered it more, the idea of UFOs does fit perfectly with Satan's lie and his plan to deceive mankind in your day.

There is no question that if a UFO landed on earth, or if we had some kind of first contact, it would instantly change our entire understanding of the universe. Former U.S. President Ronald Reagan speculated on such a theory during one of his speeches:

> I've often wondered, what if all of us in the world discovered that we were threatened by an outer power, from outer space, from another planet. Wouldn't we all, all of a sudden, find we didn't have any differences between us at all?[14]

Indeed, Reagan made references to UFOs on 18 different occasions. When he left the White House, he admitted to actually seeing a UFO while he was the governor of California.

Other prominent leaders in world history who have seen UFOs or believed in their existence, include Senator Barry Goldwater, Prince Philip of England, General Douglas MacArthur, John Kennedy, Jimmy Carter, and astronaut Gordon Cooper.

> The variety of witnesses of UFOs is endless. They include military personnel from the airforce, navy and marine corps. Radar specialists, aeronautical engineers, airport traffic controllers, astronomers, FBI agents, state, county and city police. Pilots and crews from American, United, Eastern, Pan American, Northwest, Western and TWA were also on the list of witnesses. Millions in the United Kingdom, France, Australia, South America, Mexico, and other nations around the world have seen UFOs.[15]

Ufology was once a comical subject, and those who claimed contact with UFOs were candidates to be locked up in a mental institution. But today some scientists are taking the possibility of the existence of life on other planets seriously. After all, if we have our own space shuttles, the idea of space travel is not so farfetched.

In 1982 NASA launched a 100-million-dollar project to seek out extraterrestrials in our universe. The project was known as SETI (Search for Extraterrestrial

Intelligence). Radio and computer equipment was placed in the Mojave Desert for several years, but no contact was ever made.

There Is Something Going On

Though nothing was discovered through SETI, government files are filled with reports of sightings of unknown objects. The evidence gathered and accounts by credible eyewitnesses indicate that something is going on out there.

But are the sightings really UFOs, or could there be another explanation? Don't forget that seducing spirits have a certain free rein in our day and an even greater one in yours. In this kind of environment, you don't want to believe everything you see.

Dr. Jacques Vallee was an astrophysicist by training and a computer scientist by profession. He spent over three decades studying ufology. After investigating virtually every claim of UFO sightings or extraterrestrial contact, Vallee came to the conclusion that UFOs were probably a reality but they didn't appear to be physical.

He also discovered that the phenomena involved in ufology was virtually the same as the phenomena involved with the paranormal and the occult. Dr. Vallee is not a Christian spouting off the evils of some cult. He is a scientist and a believer in UFOs. In his book *Messengers of Deception*, he noted:

> A few investigators—notably Ray Palmer, John Keel, and Salvatore Freixedo—have suggested both in public statements and in private

conversations with me that there may be a link between UFO events and "occult" phenomena.

At first view, the very suggestion of such a link is disturbing to a scientist. However . . . the phenomena reported by [UFO] witnesses involve poltergeist effects, levitation, psychic control, healing and out-of-body experiences . . . familiar [themes] . . . [of] occult literature . . . found in the teachings of the Rosicrucian Order, [etc.] . . . which have inspired not only the witchcraft revival, but also . . . "psychic" writers and . . . "scientific parapsychologists." . . . Furthermore, there is a connection between UFOs and occult themes in their social effects.[16]

Almost a decade later, Vallee wrote in *Dimensions: A Casebook of Alien Contact:*

In the last twenty-five years, at least ten thousand sightings of unidentified flying objects have been filed away unexplained by competent investigators (I am not referring here to the number of cases reported but only to those unsolved, and my figure is a conservative one), but no bridge has yet been built between this body of data and the evidence that exists for psychic phenomena such as precognition, psychokinesis, and telepathy. Such a bridge is needed, not only because current research on parapsychology could shed light on some of the more mystifying UFO incidents, but also because in return, an understanding of the nature of the UFO phenomenon could provide new insights into unusual events that have not yet been duplicated in the laboratory. It would give a clue to the mechanism of some psychic processes. . . .

What happens if we examine the files of sightings with an open mind regarding such psychic components? We find that phenomena of precognition, telepathy, and even healing are not unusual among the reports, especially when they involve close-range observation of an object or direct exposure to its light.[17]

Isn't it interesting that the same phenomena being used to prove to man that he is a god is also at the heart of these supposed space brothers? It all fits so well. You have to admit that it at least suggests a common source.

UFOs Are Not a Joke Anymore

Consider all of this in relation to a trend that has taken place over the last few decades. Whitley Strieber in the mid-1980s wrote two books titled *Communion* and *Transformation*. These books were runaway bestsellers and sparked a new level of interest in UFOs and their purposes. Like Vallee, Strieber is not a Christian but a writer of horror novels and an alleged victim of multiple abductions by extraterrestrials.

In fact, it is worth noting that the entire focus of UFO enthusiasts today centers around reports of multitudes of people being beamed aboard UFOs. It's amazing how the reports of supposed contact have evolved from distant sightings to the point where many people now claim to have been "beamed up."

In *Communion* Strieber wrote:

> Seeming encounters with nonhuman beings are not new; they have a history dating back thousands of years. What is new in this latter part of the twentieth century is that the encounters have taken on an intensity never before experienced by humankind. . . . What may have been orchestrated with great care has not been so much a reality of the experience as public perception of it. First the craft were seen from a distance in the forties and fifties. Then they began to be observed at closer and closer range. By the early sixties there were many reports of entities, and a few abduction cases. Now in the mid-eighties, I and others—for the most part independent of one another—have begun to discover this presence [abduction by an extraterrestrial] in our lives.[18]

E.T., Who Are You?

In *Communion*, Strieber recounts the details of an evening in which his wife, son, and a friend all saw the same phenomenon at the same time. This would seem to suggest that something other than hallucinations in the mind of one person is at play. As Christians we believe demons to be responsible. Interestingly, Strieber also entertained the thought of this possibility. However, he believed the demon to be part of the human psyche rather than a separate entity as the Bible claims. In *Transformation* he suggested:

> All of these beings—grays and blonds alike—fit the ancient notions of demons, angels, and "little people." I reflected that the greater part of my knowledge had come from the gray beings. The word *demon* is derived from the Greek *daimon*, which is roughly synonymous with *soul*. . . . This led me back to something else I had noticed about the visitor experience. From the experiences of people like Mrs. Sharp and from dozens of the letters that were pouring in, it was clear that the soul was very much at issue. People experienced feeling as if their souls were being dragged from their bodies. I'd had an incident of total separation of soul and body. More than one person had seen the visitors in the context of a near-death experience. "We recycle souls," they had said.[19]

Jacques Vallee also noted the connection between the UFO world and the spirit world:

> Some witnesses have thought they had seen demons because the creature had the unpredictability and mischievousness associated with popular conceptions of the devil. If you wanted to bypass the intelligentsia and church, remain undetectable to the military system, leave undisturbed the political and administrative

levels of a society, and at the same time implant deep within that society far-reaching doubts concerning its basic philosophical tenets, this is exactly how you would have to act. At the same time, of course, such a process *would have to provide its own explanation* to make ultimate detection impossible. In other words, it would have to project an image just beyond the belief structure of the target society. *It would have to disturb and reassure at the same time, exploiting both the gullibility of the zealots and the narrow-mindedness of the debunkers.* This is exactly what the UFO phenomenon does.[20]

So there is something at work here. A new idea is sweeping through our world setting the stage for yours. It is an idea with the power to change the way the entire world thinks and believes. All that would be needed is some kind of convincing, believable encounter. Before we move on, we would like you to consider the following two quotes by Whitley Strieber and Jacques Vallee:

> It is a social issue of the utmost importance, because it has all the potential of a truly powerful idea to enter unconscious mythology and there to generate beliefs so broad in their scope and deep in their impact that they emerge with religious implications for the surrounding culture.
>
> The only thing now needed to make the UFO myth a new religion of remarkable scope and force is a single undeniable sighting.[21]

I think the stage is set for the appearance of new faiths, centered on the UFO belief. To a greater degree than all the phenomena modern science is confronting, the UFO can inspire awe, the sense of the smallness of man, and an idea of the possibility of contact with the cosmic. The religions we have briefly surveyed began with the miraculous experiences of one person, but today there are thousands for whom the belief in otherworldly contact is based on intimate conviction, drawn from what they regard as personal contact with UFOs and their occupants. The phenomena and its effects are working here as they have worked at Fatima and Lourdes and in other places: as a spiritual control system.[22]

CHAPTER SIX

WHY YOU SHOULDN'T TAKE THE MARK

Throughout this book Patti and I have taken great pains to remind you that when we talk about the world in which you are living, we are looking through a prism of time. This means we cannot see everything with complete clarity. We think that part of the reason for this is that many of the Bible's prophetic passages were written to help us understand God's plan in general, and at the same time they were written specifically for you. You will see their meaning in a way we never could.

However, as we have also seen, there are some areas where the Lord gives far more specific detail than in others. One of these is something that we know as the mark of the beast. Of course, it will be known as something quite different in your world.

Before we go any further, we think that the best thing may be for us to simply quote one of the passages from the Bible that speaks of this mark. So much of it speaks for itself that if this is already being implemented in your world, we're sure you will recognize it immediately:

> And he causeth all, both small and great, rich and poor, free and bond, to receive a mark in their right hand or in their foreheads, and that no man might buy or sell, save he that had the mark, or the name of the beast, or the number of his name (Revelation 13:16,17).

Simply stated, the Bible told us 2000 years ago that a system would evolve in your day in which no one on the entire planet would be able to buy or sell anything unless they had a mark in their right hand or forehead. The idea of tracking the buying and selling everyone on the planet does was considered an impossible task. In fact, for the first 1500 years after the book of Revelation was written early in the first century, the world did not even know that North, Central, and South America existed!

But we all know how different that is now, both in our world and yours. We have both lived in a time of tremendous technological growth where communication anywhere on the globe is almost instantaneous. The global economy has been born, multinational corporations dominate the economies of diverse countries and cultures, and smart cards and electronic transactions have replaced barter and most cash transactions. Perhaps by your time cash has already become obsolete.

The point is this: Since everything electronic is traceable, the technology now exists to have a system that could track the buying and selling done by every person on the planet. And at the same time, the idea of implanting a microchip in people for identification is gaining acceptance. Let us give you just a few examples of the types of things being written in our day. The first comes from Martin Anderson of the Hoover Institute and the second from Terry Galanoy, the former director of communications for what is today Visa International:

> You see, there is an identification system made by the Hughes Aircraft Company that you can't lose. It's a syringe implantable transponder. According to promotional literature, it is an "ingenious, safe, inexpensive, foolproof, and permanent method of . . . identification using radio waves." A tiny microchip, the size of a grain of rice, is simply placed under the skin. It is so designed as to be injected simultaneously with a vaccination or alone.[1]

> Protesting too loudly about it isn't going to help either, because the disturbance you kick up is going to end up in one of your files. And on the come-and-get-it day when we're all totally and completely dependent upon our

card—or whatever survival device might replace it—you might be left all alone without one! [2]

Today's Ideas Will Be Your Reality

Of course, these ideas are only suggestions in our day. Such a system, based on a mark in the right hand or forehead, will not happen until your time, after the Antichrist has risen on the world scene. After all, according to the Bible, it is *his* mark.

We could take great lengths to speak to you about how technology makes this all possible. In fact, my brother Paul and I wrote a book for people on this side of the rapture called *Racing Toward the Mark of the Beast* (Harvest House Publishers, 1994) which looked at all of this in great detail. Patti and I don't feel that we should repeat that information because we think you will see this all happen right before your very eyes. No, there is something much more important that we need to share. If all that was involved here was the technology to speed up banking and make personal identification more secure, then God would not have gone into such detail on explaining this "mark." And that is the first clue.

Much More Than an Economic Decision

God's primary concern is not that the Antichrist is going to conquer the world or consolidate all of the banking and financial interests. That is not what this is about. It's about souls. It's about *your* soul. That is what the whole battle is being waged over. In both God's eyes and Satan's, your soul is more precious than all the riches of the earth. This is why the mark of the beast is not about economics or technology. This is just the technique, the tool used by Satan and his Antichrist to carry out the real game plan. Listen to the warning God has written especially for you:

> If any man worship the beast and his image, and receive his mark in his forehead or in his hand, the same shall drink of the wine of the wrath of God, which is poured out without mixture. . . . And the smoke of their torment ascendeth up for ever and ever; and they have no rest day or night, who worship the beast and his image, and whosoever receiveth the mark of his name (Revelation 14:9-11).

Do you see the eternal implications of that decision? Suddenly you can see, as few on our side of the rapture seem to understand, that this is not about economics at all. Certainly, God would not condemn people to eternal punishment because they chose MasterCard over Visa or made some other innocuous decision. This is something far bigger. So let's take a moment and put this back in context—a context that we are sure will be all too real to you.

Stand Up and Be Counted

You will notice in the above passage how God stressed that the decision to take this mark would be intricately tied to the worship of the Antichrist and his image. As such, it seems that a person's decision to take the mark will be a sign or a symbol that he agrees with this great world leader and the direction that he is leading. The closest example we can come up with is the "heil Hitler" salute used in Nazi Germany. In essence, this mark will be a very practical, very useful, very strict way of ensuring who is on the Antichrist's side and who is not. It will be the pledge of allegiance to the beast and his new world order.

As we've already shared, Revelation 13 describes the Antichrist's rise on the world scene in some detail. Let's remember his platform, the words that come out of his mouth:

> And there was given unto him a mouth speaking great things and blasphemies; and power was given unto him to continue forty and two months. And he opened his mouth in blasphemy against God, to blaspheme his name, and his tabernacle, and them that dwell in heaven. And it was given unto him to make war with the saints, and to overcome them; and power was given him over all kindreds, and tongues, and nations (Revelation 13:5-7).

Will the world accept this tirade of hate? You already know the answer because you have seen it happen. We know the answer because, as incredulous as it sounds, the Bible has already told us the world's reaction:

> And they worshipped the dragon
> which gave power unto the beast, and they
> worshipped the beast, saying, Who is like
> unto the beast? Who is able to make war
> with him? . . . And all that dwell upon the
> earth shall worship him, whose names are
> not written in the book of life of the Lamb
> slain from the foundation of the world
> (Revelation 13:4,8).

So what do we have here? We have a leader ris-
ing on the world scene whose primary message is
hatred toward God—a leader who openly declares
war on the saints of God. And we have the entire
world not only agreeing with him, but also worshiping him and even worshiping Lucifer directly.
It sounds incredible from our side of the rapture,
but we know it will be a shocking reality on your
side. At the same time, in the midst of all this there
is the mark of the beast—the symbol of those who
accept this leader and his plan.

You Face a Decision

The acceptance of this mark of allegiance, we are
sure, will be the result of a personal, conscious spiritual submission that a person makes to the beast.
How compelling it will be is seen in the wording
above. Virtually everyone on the face of the earth
will succumb to the charms of this great deceiver.
Only those who commit to following God will
escape. Only those whose minds are protected by
God Himself will be able to overcome the deception:

> For there shall arise false Christs, and
> false prophets, and shall show great signs
> and wonders; insomuch that, if it were
> possible, they shall deceive the very elect.
> Behold, I have told you before (Matthew
> 24:24,25).

Those who choose the mark (for no one will be
forced to take it) will not want it only so that they
can buy and sell. They will want it because they
have said in their hearts, "We believe in this man.
We believe in the solutions he offers. We believe that
if we eliminate the outmoded ideas of God and sin,
we can have global peace and harmony. We believe
he is a god!"

In this light, we can understand why God will
pour out such judgment on those who receive the
mark. It is not because of the mark itself but because
of the spiritual decision that underlies it.

How Will He Do It?

In our world, 666 is probably the most infamous
of all numbers. It's in movies, songs, books—every-
where you can imagine. Music promoters use it to
shock and show defiance. Writers use it to symbolize
evil, and movie producers use it to frighten their
audiences to tears.

But in every instance, everyone knows that this
number, 666, is the number of the devil. So then the
question is, "How is this beast going to get everyone
in the world to reject God and accept the very number that everyone knows is the devil's number?"

From our vantage point, we can only guess. You probably already know.

We think (and we may well be wrong) that one possibility could be this: The Antichrist is openly speaking blasphemies against God, His Word, and His tabernacle. The beast is the pinnacle of arrogance in using supposed miraculous demonstrations. He is a charmer. He could try to use all of his charm and magical powers to snare people.

The Antichrist may tell you that you have been deceived and in bondage for too long to religious mythology and negative, intolerant traditions. The argument could be along these lines:

> We can no longer tolerate such narrow-minded and superstitious thinking in our new world of peace and harmony. We must all come together and demonstrate the success of our new world. We must not be paralyzed by superstitions and kept from the next step in our spiritual evolution. To prove that we are not frightened by these "old wives' tales," we'll openly accept the challenge of failed Christianity and take for ourselves and our new world order the very symbol these religious fanatics have erroneously associated with something sinister. We'll take 666 as our own!

No matter how good the plan sounds, no matter how logical the ideas of global harmony are, and no matter how difficult it will be to live in your world without the mark, please stop and realize that what is at the heart of this empire (and the mark representing it) is a clear rejection of God and an acceptance of a false religious system—a false system that will cost you your very soul.

God is able to lead and guide you and give you eternal life. All you have to do is accept that offer with an open heart. The road will not be easy. But the rewards will be eternal. Don't forget: As compelling as the lies all sound, the Lord did tell us what this deception would be. Jesus encourages you: "Behold, I have told you before."

CHAPTER SEVEN

WHERE ARE YOU NOW IN HISTORY?

Up until this point we have shared with you information on the time in which you find yourself living. We have warned you about the false leaders and false teachings they will spread. We've even told you why this time had to come before Jesus could return to earth. But now we want to try to explain to you exactly where you are in God's time schedule and what lies ahead. According to the Bible, world history—including the time in which you live—has been broken down into several relatively distinct stages.

In its most general sense, we saw the period from

the time of creation until Jesus Christ as the Old Testament age. During this time period, God's dealings were centered largely on the nation of Israel. The Old Testament period came to an end with the birth or first coming of Jesus Christ, and His crucifixion, resurrection, and ascension into heaven.

The New Testament age, or the church age as it is also known, began on the day of Pentecost when God filled the disciples with His Holy Spirit. This is the day when a new period really began. From that day forward, God began dealing with a new entity called "the church." Now the church, according to the Bible, is not a building or an organization. The church is made up of every believer in Jesus Christ. This includes everyone from the apostles Paul and Peter, to Billy Graham, to Patti and me. It includes every believer, whether that person has been buried for centuries or is alive now in our time.

From the day of Pentecost until today as we write these words to you, mankind has been in the church age. But that age ended when the event called the rapture took place. You now live in yet another age.

Pinpointing Where You Are on God's Time Line

Unlike Patti and I, who only know that we are at some point near the end of the church age, we can pinpoint exactly where you are on God's time line for planet earth. This is because you live in a time when God is back to dealing primarily with Israel (though He will still lead you as well, if you let Him). During His dealings with Israel, God has given some very specific time lines on which events can be calculated. In our age, the church age, God gave no such detail. He told us that His coming to "snatch" us away would come as a surprise, and that we should always be ready. In fact, the only reason that we knew the rapture was even close was because we were beginning to see the stage being set for the fulfillment of prophecies related to His return to earth at the end of the seven-year period in which you now live. Our reasoning was simple. If everything was falling into place for Jesus to return to earth, and the rapture was to come seven years earlier, we knew the time was at hand.

Perhaps the best place to start in our explanation of all this is back at the time of a Hebrew prophet we have already mentioned. His name was Daniel, and he lived in Israel and Babylon about 2500 years ago. Daniel was a man so close to God that the Lord showed him the future in great detail, including how to calculate the exact date when Jesus would first come to present Himself as Israel's Messiah and the exact date when He would return to earth the second time.

At the time, the nation of Israel was in captivity in Babylon. Daniel, who had been brought to Babylon, was praying to God and asking Him what He planned to do with Israel, God's chosen people. Daniel was asking God about the next few weeks and months, but God wanted to explain to His beloved servant the whole story. So instead He told Daniel what He planned to do with Daniel's people (Israel) throughout history.

The pinpoint detail that the Lord revealed to Daniel is absolutely staggering. And what He has chosen to reveal to you today through that same prophecy is even more dramatic. You see, God through Daniel has given you (though not Patti and me) the ability to calculate the date of Jesus' return to earth. Through what is known as the prophecy of the 70 weeks, you can also know the day on which the great leader who has arisen on the world scene will show his true colors. I think you will have to agree with us that this is very solid proof that God is indeed alive and well, even in this time of darkness in which you live.

Let's look at this prophecy together. Daniel was told that a period of 490 years (each of the 70 weeks equals 7 years*) would pass and then Israel's sins would come to an end. She would enter an age of everlasting righteousness and accept her Messiah (Daniel chapter 9).

"But wait a minute," you may be saying. "If you start from a period of about 2500 years ago when Daniel lived and add 490 years you only come to about 2000 B.C. There is no way these things took place then. In fact, they still haven't taken place in my day or yours. How can this be?"

Well, the answer lies in the fact that the 490 years were broken down into different parts. Here is the exact wording from the book of Daniel, including the event that would mark the time at which the counting should begin:

---

* In the time in which this is written, Israelis referred to periods of seven years as a week of years all the time. This was a common and accepted reference, though it seems a little odd to us today.

Seventy weeks are determined upon thy
people. . . . Know therefore and understand, that from the going forth of the
commandment to restore and to build
Jerusalem unto the Messiah the Prince shall
be seven weeks, and threescore and two
weeks; the street shall be built again, and
the wall, even in troublous times. And after
threescore and two weeks shall Messiah be
cut off, but not for himself (Daniel 9:24-26).

The first thing we would ask you to do is count
the weeks here. You will notice that they only add
up to 69 weeks (7 plus 60 plus 2). Thus, what we are
being told at this point is that from the time of the
commandment to restore and rebuild Jerusalem
(remember, Daniel had just seen it destroyed and
was in captivity in Babylon), until the coming of the
Messiah would be 69 weeks, or 483 years.

It was also revealed to Daniel that at the end of
that 483 years, the Messiah would be "cut off, but
not for himself." What a perfect description of the
death that Jesus died on the cross. He was indeed
cut off, but not for Himself. He died for us. He died
that we might have eternal life, if only we believed.

Calculations from Scotland Yard

Sir Robert Anderson, born in Dublin, Ireland, in
1841, was a well-known lay preacher and wrote several bestselling books on biblical subjects. But
Anderson was more than just a preacher. In 1863 he
became a member of the Irish Bar where he served

on the legal circuit. In 1888, the same year that the infamous Jack the Ripper was terrorizing London, Anderson joined Scotland Yard as the chief of the Criminal Investigation Department.

His skills as a Scotland Yard detective also helped Anderson in his research and investigation of biblical subjects. In his book *The Coming Prince*, Anderson calculated the exact date of that commandment to rebuild Jerusalem, and then calculated the day which fell exactly 483 years later. The detective wrote:

> The blessings promised to Judah and Jerusalem were postponed till after a period described as "seventy weeks"; and at the close of the sixty-ninth week of this era the Messiah should be "cut off." These seventy weeks represent seventy times seven prophetic years of 360 days [the length of the Jewish calendar year], to be reckoned from the issuing of an edict for the rebuilding of the city—"the street and rampart," of Jerusalem.
>
> The edict in question was the decree issued by Artaxerxes Longimanus in the twentieth year of his reign, authorising Nehemiah to rebuild the fortifications of Jerusalem. The date of Artaxerxes's reign can be definitely ascertained—not from elaborate disquisitions by biblical commentators and prophetic writers, but by the united voice of secular historians and chronologers.[1]

Anderson's investigation led him to the date of the first of Nisan, 445 B.C., or March 14, as the date that the Persian ruler Artaxerxes gave the edict to restore Judah's autonomy and rebuild Jerusalem.

The true impact of what we are talking about doesn't become evident until we count forward 483 biblical years or 173,880 days. This takes us to the date of the tenth of Nisan, or April 6, A.D. 32. Well, history confirms that April 6, A.D. 32 is a very significant date. Indeed, on that exact date an event took place which is actually recorded in the Gospel of Luke. In chapter 19, starting at verse 37 we read:

> And when He was come nigh, even now at the descent of the mount of Olives, the whole multitude of the disciples began to rejoice and praise God with a loud voice for all the mighty works that they had seen; saying, Blessed be the King that cometh in the name of the Lord; peace in heaven, and glory in the highest. And some of the Pharisees from among the multitude said unto him, Master, rebuke thy disciples. And he answered and said unto them, I tell you that, if these should hold their peace, stones would immediately cry out. And when he was come near, he beheld the city, and wept over it, saying, if thou hadst known, even thou, at least in this thy day, the things which belong unto thy peace! But now they are hid from thine eyes.

Anderson concludes:

> What then was the length of the period intervening between the issuing of the decree

to rebuild Jerusalem and the public advent of "Messiah the Prince,"—between the 14th March, B.C. 445, and the 6th April, A.D. 32? *The interval contained exactly and to the very day 173,880 days, or seven times sixty-nine prophetic years of 360 days,* the first sixty-nine weeks of Gabriel's prophecy.[2]

However, we know that at the end of this 483-year period Israel didn't receive her Messiah. Instead, she rejected and crucified Him. When she did this, God literally stopped the 490-year time clock He had set for Israel while there were still seven biblical years (or 2520 days) left.

At this point God turned His attention to a new entity called the church. As we explained earlier, Patti and I are a part of that church which is made up of everyone who has ever accepted Jesus Christ as Lord and Savior. Some of us are still living on this earth. Many more have died—or as the Bible puts it, have fallen asleep. This is why the Lord was so specific in promising that both those that "sleep" and those who are alive will be caught up "together" in the great disappearance we await and which you have witnessed.

> For this we say unto you by the word of the Lord, that we which are alive and remain unto the coming of the Lord shall not prevent them which are asleep. For the Lord himself shall descend from heaven with a shout, with the voice of the archangel, and with the trump of God, and

the dead in Christ shall rise first. Then we which are alive and remain shall be caught up together with them in the clouds to meet the Lord in the air, and so shall we ever be with the Lord (1 Thessalonians 4:15-17).

You Know the Day—We Don't!

There is something important that you need to understand. There was no defining time frame given in God's Word for how long this church age would last. God's time clock is only concerned with Israel. The church age was an interruption in this precise time line. He never told us how long it would be. So we don't know when Jesus will return to earth.

We know it will happen at the end of the final seven biblical years (2520 days), but we don't know when these seven years start. But you do because they have already begun!

If the clock stopped when Israel rejected her Messiah and God turned His attention to the new entity called the church, then doesn't it make sense that the clock started again at exactly the time when the church disappeared? So this means that you know the exact date when Jesus will return to this earth to set up His kingdom just as He promised the prophet Daniel. All you have to do is take the date of the rapture and add seven biblical years (2520 days). This will be the day Jesus returns to the earth at the height of a battle called the Battle of Armageddon. And as we will show you in the next chapter, this same prophecy also makes it possible to understand when another key event will take place, causing God's full judgments to begin to fall on the earth. So let's begin to look at what lies ahead. . . .

CHAPTER EIGHT

WHAT'S GOING ON IN THE MIDDLE EAST?

In the last chapter, we told you about the prophecy of the 70 weeks from the book of Daniel. It was this prophecy that allowed us to show you how you can calculate exactly where you are on history's time clock. You will also recall that we told you this prophecy indicated there are still seven years remaining on God's prophetic time clock.

The Lord has given us another set of circumstances that center around the seven years remaining on God's prophetic time clock. Let's take a look at the last verse of the prophecy of the 70 weeks:

> And he [the Antichrist] shall confirm
> the covenant with many for one week; and
> in the midst of the week he shall cause the
> sacrifice and the oblation to cease, and for
> the overspreading of abominations he
> shall make it desolate, even until the con-
> summation, and that determined shall be
> poured upon the desolate (Daniel 9:27).

This verse is full of difficult language that probably doesn't seem to make a lot of sense at first.
Let's examine some of the pieces so that you can
begin to understand.

First, you will notice that this passage once again
makes reference to a period of one week. This reference should be familiar to you now. We understand
that this is the final seven-year period when God is
once again focusing on the nation of Israel now that
the church is gone. This is the time in which you are
living.

However, there is an important implication here.
It seems likely that since the Antichrist confirms this
covenant for a period of precisely seven years, then
this confirmation will probably occur right at the very
beginning of the seven-year tribulation period. This
means it is an event that will probably occur at the
same time as the other event that will mark the beginning of the final seven-year countdown: the rapture!*

---

* Some scholars believe that there may be a slight gap in time
between the rapture and the treaty. If so, the timing of the second
coming would still be counted from the date of the rapture.
However, the date of the "abomination of desolation" we refer to in
the next chapter would be counted from the date of the treaty.

It is for this very reason that, as students of Bible prophecy on this side of the rapture, we watch the developments in the Middle East very carefully. You see, we believe that a very significant portion of the fulfillment of this prophecy will center around a peace treaty between Israel and "the many" enemies she has. As we watch the nations of the world struggle to come up with a solution for the Mideast dilemma, we know that at some point a seven-year deal will be proposed. This is exciting because, while there are no signs given to tell us when the rapture will take place, if these two events do take place at roughly the same time, then we can sort of gauge how close we may be to the rapture.

However, much more important is the fact that the Lord has given you major proof of His foreknowledge right here because, if Patti and I understand it correctly, you are witnessing the beginnings of that very treaty right now. You are living in the moments spoken of by the prophets and discussed among Bible students throughout the centuries.

Israel at the Center of This New World Order

We want to remind you that this entire prophecy is about Daniel's people—Israel. Given the fact that this verse speaks about Jewish worship rituals (the sacrifice, the oblations, and the covenant), there is little question that Israel is at the center of "the many." But the implication of "the many" is that many more nations are involved. In fact, we have long speculated that this treaty will actually be something along the lines of a "Constitution of the New

World Order." We think it may be a global peace treaty which is based on peace in the Middle East.

Now we may be dead wrong on this, but we do know from this passage and others that the treaty will contain at least the following provisions:

1. The Antichrist will allow Israel to reinstate temple worship. This implies he will allow Israel to rebuild her temple (something very problematic in our day since the Moslem Holy Place—the Dome of the Rock—today sits on the Temple Mount).
2. The duration of the treaty will be seven years.
3. Israel will be guaranteed the military protection of the Antichrist's armies.*

Implicit in bringing peace between Israel and her enemies is bringing peace between Israel and the Arabs. Could it really happen? We believe that by your day the answer will be yes, at least temporarily. Don't forget that this is no small task you are witnessing. It has never happened before. And you now know who brought it about. By the Bible's own warning, you know that whoever achieved it is not Christ, as many will say, but Antichrist!

Back to the Future

To try to put this whole Israel/new world order connection into perspective, let us skip ahead to the

---

* We know this from chapter 38 of the book of Ezekiel which tells us that Israel will lay down all of her arms and become a land of "unwalled villages."

end of this seven-year tribulation period when Jesus Himself will return to earth. There are several reasons why we would like to do this. The first is that the Bible gives us some detail on Christ's return and the context of that return, while less detail is given on the Antichrist's rise to power. And since, as we've shared, the Antichrist is a counterfeit of the true Christ, if we understand the coming of Christ, then great light will also be shed on the coming of His impostor.

Here's what we know about the return of Jesus at the end of the seven years:

1. He comes at the height of a great battle called Armageddon.
2. He rescues Israel just before she is destroyed by the armies of the earth.
3. Israel recognizes Jesus as her Messiah.
4. Jesus brings peace to the earth.
5. Jesus establishes His kingdom, a 1000-year reign of peace on earth.
6. He establishes His throne in Israel, which becomes the center of the earth.

With this basic outline in mind, let's hop back to the rise of the Antichrist at the beginning of the seven years. The impostor wants to take Jesus' place. So what does he do? We figure that he will replace the millennium with his new world order. And where does he center his activities? Israel! But then the question is raised, "Will Israel accept him as Messiah?"

Here's what Jesus said to the Jews on the day they rejected Him as their Messiah:

I am come in my Father's name, and ye
receive me not; if another shall come in his
own name, him ye will receive (John 5:43).

Jesus was warning the spiritually blinded children of Israel that a counterfeit would indeed come,
and they would receive him with open arms. Today,
we can understand how it could happen. Patti and I
have spent a great deal of time in Israel and have
seen the ravages of war and terrorism. We have
talked to people there and asked them how they
would recognize the Messiah if He came. Almost to
the person they respond, "He will bring peace."

This breaks our hearts because the Bible is very
clear that this is the very thing the Antichrist will
use to deceive them. The prophet Daniel tells us "by
peace [he will] destroy many" (8:25). However, the
Antichrist's impersonation runs much deeper than
this. This is why we believe the "covenant" will
include a peace plan for the whole earth, because
this is what Jesus brings when He comes. We also
believe that the timing of the rapture and this treaty
may coincide with a devastating attack on Israel,
during which the Antichrist will seemingly rescue
her, once again to duplicate the coming of the true
Messiah. This guy may even point to the Scriptures
and claim to be fulfilling them. Don't believe it. He
comes in his own name.

Who is a liar but he that denieth that
Jesus is the Christ? He is antichrist, that
denieth the Father and the Son (1 John 2:22).

Preparation for Peace

One of the obvious preconditions for Israel signing such a peace covenant would be her need of peace. Anyone living in our present world, and more than likely in yours, could not deny that this has been the desire of Israel. Since she became a nation on May 14, 1948, Israel has been surrounded by neighboring Arab enemies wishing to push her into the sea. In fact, on the very day that she became a nation, Israel was attacked by several neighboring Arab nations.

Since then she has been in a constant state of war with virtually all of the Arab states. At the time of writing this book, only two Arab nations, Egypt and Jordan, are formally at peace with Israel. And the Palestinians have a tentative agreement to make peace with Israel.

In 1979 Egypt's President Anwar Sadat signed a peace treaty at Camp David with Israeli Prime Minister Menachem Begin. Sadat was assassinated shortly thereafter. Since that time until 1993, Israel remained at war with most of the other Arab nations. Then on September 13, 1993, Israel signed a Declaration of Principles with the PLO, once known as the terrorist Palestine Liberation Organization. During secret meetings in Oslo, Norway, the PLO and Israeli Foreign Minister Shimon Peres came to an agreement to work on a phased plan for Palestinian self-rule. A final agreement for phased planning was reached in Cairo, Egypt, on May 4, 1994.

In this agreement the PLO was recognized by the Israeli government as the voice for the Palestinian people. The agreement also gave the Palestinians limited self-rule in Gaza and Jericho over administrative positions like education, welfare, and a police force. This was to be an initial step in what was hoped would lead to peace with the Palestinians, and perhaps autonomy over their own region. This was not a peace treaty but a step toward peace.

And then on July 25, 1994, Israel also came to an agreement with Jordan. Israeli Prime Minister Yitzhak Rabin and King Hussein of Jordan shook hands publicly for the first time on the White House lawn and jointly signed the Washington Declaration with U.S. President Bill Clinton witnessing the event. A full and official peace treaty between the two nations was signed on October 26, 1994.

In the text of the declaration reached in July 1994, we read:

> After generations of hostility, blood, and tears and in the wake of years of pain and wars, His Majesty King Hussein and Prime Minister Yitzhak Rabin are determined to bring an end to bloodshed and sorrow. Jordan and Israel aim at the achievement of just, lasting, and comprehensive peace between Israel and its neighbors and at the conclusion of a Treaty of Peace between both countries. . . .
>
> Following the declaration and in keeping with the Agreed Common Agenda both countries will refrain from actions or activities by either side that may adversely affect the security of the other or may prejudice the final outcome of negotiations. Neither side will threaten the other by use

of force, weapons, or any other means against each other and both sides will thwart threats to security resulting from all kinds of terrorism.[1]

None of these declarations or treaties were the treaty of the Antichrist that is to usher in the tribulation period. They were instead the beginning of the final process. Unfortunately, Patti and I believe that these efforts will lead to war and not peace in the Middle East. Already, extremists are blowing up everything in sight to try to derail the process. But there is a more significant reason for our doubts concerning peace in the Middle East. The Bible indicates in Isaiah 19 that true peace will not come to this region until Jesus returns. Moreover, the Bible indicates a false peace will arise under the fake messiah. If man could solve his own problems, he would not need a miracle worker to do it, right? So, we speculate that the false peace will emerge out of the ashes of failed diplomacy and warfare.

The Division of Land

There is something else very important to this whole situation that we want to point out. We know that the Antichrist will "divide the land for gain" during his reign in the tribulation period (Daniel 11:39). In the Bible "the land" always refers to Israel.

Interestingly, the "land for peace" issue between Israel and her Arab neighbors is very big in our time of history. In its declaration with the PLO, Israel allowed the Palestinians limited self-rule in Gaza and Jericho, with the intention of this leading to full autonomy in these areas as well as other areas in the West Bank.

Negotiations have also been ongoing with Syria, but these are at somewhat of a standstill at the time we are writing this book. Syrian President Hafez Assad (coined by one Israeli journalist as the Frank Sinatra of the Middle East because he wants it his way) will not budge unless Israel meets his full demands. Interestingly, these demands center around Israel giving up land for peace. Syria has said it will not discuss peace until Israel agrees to fully withdraw from the Golan Heights and southern Lebanon.

In essence, what the Palestinians and Syrians are demanding is that Israel return to its pre-1967 borders. During the Six-Day War lasting from June 5 to 10, 1967, Israel defeated the combined forces of Egypt, Syria, Iraq, and Jordan. In its victory Israel took control of the Sinai,* Gaza, Judea and Samaria, the Golan Heights, and East Jerusalem.

However, the thought of Israel returning to her original 1967 borders seems impossible today. The land that she took control of in self-defense during the Six-Day War has been significant to her strategic defense since. In speaking of the 1973 Yom Kippur War, Israeli politician Benjamin Netanyahu wrote:

> On both the Egyptian and Syrian fronts, the Arabs had managed to penetrate as much as twenty miles before Israeli forces finally checked them. If the war had begun

---

* In its peace treaty with Egypt, Israel agreed to return the Sinai, which it did.

not on the post-1967 lines but on the *pre-*
1967 lines, and if the Arab armies had
advanced the same distances, Israel would
have ceased to exist.[2]

While Israel would obviously be reluctant to give
up land that is strategically necessary to her existence, the Antichrist may convince her that she will
be secure even if she does give up these important
pieces of real estate. The Bible does say that Israel
will become a "land of unwalled villages" (Ezekiel
38:11). In our thinking, the current nation of Israel
would have to believe that this leader was the
Messiah before they would ever enter into such an
agreement. To us, it sounds almost unbelievable. To
you, it's probably history!

CHAPTER NINE

WHAT LIES AHEAD?

When Patti and I felt led of the Lord to write this message to you, we struggled with the question of what to include. The first thing I wanted to do was write a blow-by-blow account of every detail of the tribulation period based on the great detail given to us by the Scriptures. However, Patti in her wisdom suggested that I may be going a bit over-board. She pointed out wisely that the problem is that while such detailed commentaries may be of use for discussion purposes among theologians in our day, they have a simple flaw. And that flaw is that we are looking through that prism in time, trying to understand events that the human mind cannot fully grasp.

Watching the fulfillment of prophecy in our day has shown us one thing. While Bible prophecy after prophecy have been fulfilled right before our eyes, not all of them have come to pass in exactly the way we thought they would. We realized how careful we had to be when writing to you as someone who is actually living in the middle of our theological discussions. A better approach, we decided, would be to give you enough key points to show you that the time in which you are living was indeed prophesied. We wanted to warn you about the deceptions coming your way and what you can do to ensure your eternal salvation. And for the details, we decided to point you to the Scriptures.

However, this raised another problem. We have no idea how easily accessible these Scriptures will be in your day. By the sounds of the first address the Antichrist will give to the world, we have a feeling Bibles may be burning. Again, maybe not. Perhaps he will say, "We have just misunderstood what the Bible was meant to say."

Just to play it safe, Patti and I decided to include the best description of your time right in this book. Thus, in the Appendix you will find the book of Revelation, the last book in the Bible. You will also find one chapter from the books of Matthew and Daniel, and three from Ezekiel. These will give you a great portion of the detail of events taking place in your world. But if you can, try to find a full Bible. In there you will find "all truth."

Hitting the Main Points

Having said this, there are a few key events and chronologies that we thought we would go through to give you a framework for what lies ahead.

As we have discussed, the seven-year tribulation period began with the rapture of the church. We also believe that a seven-year treaty involving Israel (and probably most of the world) will have been brokered at roughly the same time. You will recall that the "covenant" sets a time frame of exactly seven years:

> And he [the Antichrist] shall confirm the covenant with many for one week, and in the midst of the week he shall cause the sacrifice and oblation to cease, and for the overspreading of abominations he shall make it desolate (Daniel 9:27).

There is another major event on the horizon that you need to be aware of. We know very specifically that the Antichrist will cause the temple sacrifice to cease halfway through his covenant with Israel. You can know that this will happen exactly 1260 days after the signing of this treaty.

But the Bible indicates that the Antichrist will actually do more than just that. He desecrates the Jewish temple. The obvious question you must have is, "What is the abomination of desolation that the Antichrist will perform?" The apostle Paul tells us in 2 Thessalonians 2:4 what the son of perdition (verse 3) will do. We are told that he

> opposeth and exalteth himself above all
> that is called God, or that is worshipped;
> so that he as God sitteth in the temple of
> God, showing himself that he is God.

So this is the abomination. The Antichrist will enter the temple, probably the most sacred area of the temple which is the Holy of Holies, and proclaim himself to be the Lord God.

We know that the Antichrist is worshiped from the very start of the seven-year period, but apparently a new dimension is added at this point. Perhaps this will be the time when he claims to be the only true God, or specifically, to be the God of the Bible. Whatever the case, we know that this final act of impersonation triggers the wrath of God, and a period of wrath begins on that day which lasts until the Battle of Armageddon. Jesus Himself warned of this day very clearly:

> When ye see the abomination of desolation,
> spoken of by Daniel the prophet, stand in the
> holy place (whoso readeth let him understand),
> then let them which be in Judea flee into the
> mountains, let him which is on the housetop
> not come down to take any thing out of his
> house, neither let him which is in the field
> return back to take his clothes. And woe unto
> them that are with child, and to them that give
> suck in those days! But pray ye that your flight
> be not in the winter, neither on the sabbath day,
> for then shall be great tribulation, such as was
> not since the beginning of the world to this

time, no, nor ever shall be. And except those days should be shortened, there should no flesh be saved, but for the elect's sake those days shall be shortened (Matthew 24:15-22).

So far we have referred to the seven-year tribulation period. But as you look through the book of Revelation, you will see that it is actually broken down into two three-and-a-half-year periods. The first half will be a time of relative peace and world unity. However, this abomination of desolation marks the turning point. From this time forward God begins to pour out His judgments on the beast and those that have sided with him. This time of great tribulation continues right up until the second coming of Jesus at Armageddon. The book of Revelation contains a great amount of detail regarding this time.

The Foiled Invasion of Israel

While we know conclusively that the abomination of desolation will take place at the midpoint of the seven-year tribulation period, there is another event that we think may happen at the same time, but we cannot be so sure of the timing.

The event we are speaking of is an invasion of Israel by a confederacy of predominantly Muslim nations led by Russia. This invasion is spelled out in great detail by the prophet Ezekiel (see the passages included in the Appendix). As we've just said, the timing of this invasion is uncertain in relation to other tribulation-period events. Scholars on this side of the rapture have great differences of opinion concerning this issue.

However, having said that, we believe that this invasion will take place at about the midpoint of the tribulation period and will be related directly to this abomination of desolation. We think the scenario may go something like the following.

The Russians, beginning to sense that this "messiah" is not really who he says he is, become angry that as good Marxist-Leninists they were taken in by this fraud and his religious sidekick. They will set out to show the world that this new world order doesn't need any of these silly religious trappings. They will "devise an evil thought" and launch a great invasion on the heart of the new world order—the regathered children of Israel. The attack will come as a complete surprise. Israel will see too late that she has placed her faith in one who is not truly the Messiah. But alas, she has no weapons to defend herself. As the Russians and their hordes reach the mountains of Israel, they meet an unexpected defender of the children of Abraham, Isaac, and Jacob:

> And it shall come to pass at the same time when Gog shall come up against the land of Israel, saith the Lord GOD, that my fury shall come up in my face. For in my jealousy and in the fire of my wrath have I spoken, Surely in that day there shall be a great shaking in the land of Israel. . . . And I will call for a sword against him throughout all my mountains, saith the Lord GOD; every man's sword shall be against his

brother. . . . And I will turn thee back, and
leave but the sixth part of thee . . . and will
bring thee upon the mountains of Israel
(Ezekiel 38:18,19,21; 39:2).

As we have already seen, the prophet Ezekiel
makes it clear that when God Himself destroys the
Russian-led confederacy on the mountains of
Israel, the whole world, Jew and Gentile alike, will
recognize that the God of Israel has done this.
Enraged at the worship of Israel toward the true
God, the Antichrist rushes into the rebuilt temple
and proclaims that he is God. The children of Israel
completely reject him, and so he sets about to
destroy them. However, somehow the earth helps
the children of Israel (Revelation 12:16) and they
are protected from the Antichrist's wrath. We know
that the Antichrist goes into the temple to declare
himself as God at the midpoint of the seven-year
tribulation period (Daniel 9:27). Combining this
with the fact that the Scriptures tell us that Israel
will be protected from the Antichrist for exactly
three-and-one-half years (Revelation 12:6) gives us
a good indication that this will all happen at the
midpoint of the tribulation period. The sham of the
false millennium will quickly come to an end. Now
God's judgment begins to fall on the world. The
Antichrist shifts his energies from religious deception to military might, and he and his kings destroy
the "whore." In a world gone insane because of
plagues, judgment, and chaos, men will become
more and more rebellious:

And the rest of the men which were not killed by these plagues yet repented not of the works of their hands, that they should not worship devils, and idols of gold, and silver, and brass, and stone, and of wood, which neither can see, nor hear, nor walk. Neither repented they of their murders, nor of their sorceries, nor of their fornication, nor of their thefts. . . . And men were scorched with great heat, and blasphemed the name of God, which hath power over these plagues, and they repented not to give him glory. . . . And [they] blasphemed the God of heaven because of their pains and their sores, and repented not of their deeds (Revelation 9:20,21; 16:9,11).

Finally, they will unite to complete the job that the Russians and their allies failed to accomplish. This time, instead of meeting God the Father, they will meet God the Son!

The Final Attempt at Holocaust

The tribulation period ends with all of the nations of the world gathered to try to push Israel into the sea. What Satan has tried to achieve through years of persecution, a holocaust, war after war, and finally the great invasion from the north, he will now try to achieve with his minions—the Antichrist and false prophet—and all the armies of the earth.

But our God is a faithful God. He never forgets

His promises. Just as God the Father rescued Israel at the time of the Russian-led invasion, God the Son will rescue Israel at the height of this attack. Indeed, on that day the words of Jesus will come to pass and Israel will actually be glad to see Him:

> O Jerusalem, Jerusalem, thou that killest the prophets and stonest them which are sent unto thee, how often would I have gathered thy children together, even as a hen gathereth her chicks under her wings, and ye would not! Behold, your house is left unto you desolate. For I say unto you, Ye shall not see me henceforth till ye shall say, Blessed is he that cometh in the name of the Lord (Matthew 23:37-39).

What Satan plans for evil, God will turn to good. Remember that the end of this tribulation period in which you are living marks the end of the 490 years that God had promised to Israel. Let us remind you what God said would be accomplished then:

> Seventy weeks [490 years] are determined upon thy people and upon thy holy city, to finish the transgression, and to make an end of sins, and to make reconciliation for iniquity, and to bring in everlasting righteousness, and to seal up the vision and prophecy, and to anoint the most Holy (Daniel 9:24).

According to the prophet Zechariah, writing

under the inspiration of God over 2000 years ago, the fulfillment of this prophecy is no longer than seven years away if you are reading this right after the rapture. As the nations of the earth gather to do battle against Israel and to try to finish what the Russians and their allies started, they meet an unexpected opponent and the plans of man come to an abrupt end:

> Then shall the Lord go forth, and fight against those nations, as when he fought in the day of battle. And his feet shall stand in that day upon the mount of Olives, which is before Jerusalem on the east, and the mount of Olives shall cleave in the midst thereof toward the east and toward the west, and there shall be a very great valley and half of the mountain shall remove toward the north, and half of it toward the south. . . . And the LORD shall be king over all the earth. . . . And it shall come to pass in that day, that I will seek to destroy all the nations that come against Jerusalem. And I will pour upon the house of David, and upon the inhabitants of Jerusalem, the spirit of grace and of supplications, and they shall look upon me whom they have pierced, and they shall mourn for him, as one mourneth for his only son, and shall be in bitterness for him, as one that is in bitterness for his firstborn (Zechariah 14:3,4,9; 12:9,10).

Two thousand years ago, the nation of Israel rejected Jesus as He came down from the Mount of Olives. This time, Israel will receive Him as He once again stands on the very same mount. Far from being the suffering Messiah who came to bear the sins of the world, He is now coming in power and glory to set up His everlasting kingdom, the first 1000 years of which will be right here on this earth. The prophets tell us that all of this doesn't happen until the Battle of Armageddon at the end of the final seven-year countdown. At this time of judgment, sin and transgression come to an end as the new kingdom is established. Only those whose faith is in Christ are allowed to enter. Finally, all the purposes of the 490 years will be fulfilled. Israel will have recognized her Messiah. Sin will have come to an end, and everlasting righteousness will have begun.

You Can Be a Part of This Kingdom

However, the promises of the kingdom are not just for Israel. They are for you, too, if you will believe. And by the grace of God, whether your earthly body survives until the second coming or not, you can be a part of the kingdom if you accept Jesus as your Savior. The Bible does tell us that many of you during the tribulation will pay for your faith in Jesus with your earthly lives. But God will be with you every step of the way. And if you are faithful to Him, you will be a part of one of the most exciting moments in history, at the end of this seven-year period:

And at that time shall Michael stand up . . . and at that time thy people shall be delivered, every one that shall be found written in the book. And many of them that sleep in the dust of the earth shall awake, some to everlasting life, and some to shame and everlasting contempt. And they that be wise shall shine as the brightness of the firmament; and they that turn many to righteousness as the stars for ever and ever (Daniel 12:1-3).

And I saw the thrones, and they sat upon them, and judgment was given unto them; and I saw the souls of them that were beheaded for the witness of Jesus, and for the word of God, and which had not worshipped the beast, neither his image, neither had received his mark upon their foreheads, or in their hands; and they lived and reigned with Christ a thousand years (Revelation 20:4).

There is also the possibility that you will never know death and that you will still be here on earth to enter right into the millennium and join with those who gave their lives for their faith. If this is the case, you will see the return of Jesus with your own eyes:

And I saw heaven opened, and behold a white horse; and he that sat upon him was called Faithful and True, and in righteousness he doth judge and make war. His eyes were as a flame of fire, and on his head were many crowns; and he had a name written, that no man knew, but he himself. And he was clothed with a vesture dipped in blood, and his name is called The Word of God. And the armies which were in heaven followed him upon white horses, clothed in fine linen, white and clean. And out of his mouth goeth a sharp sword, that with it he should smite the nations, and he shall rule them with a rod of iron; and he treadeth the winepress of the fierceness and wrath of Almighty God.

And he hath on his vesture and on his thigh a name written, KING OF KINGS, AND LORD OF LORDS (Revelation 19:11-16).

CHAPTER TEN

HOW CAN I BE SAVED?

If you have not taken the mark of allegiance, there *is* hope for you yet. Although it is too late for you to have been taken in the rapture, it is not too late for you to become a believer in Jesus Christ. It is not too late for you to ask Him to be your Savior so that you may spend eternity with Him. Don't forget: We are talking about a decision of eternal consequences. The seven-year period you are now living in is but a speck of time, quickly passing away. And, even though the tribulation period in which you are living is the most deceptive and evil period of any time in history, God's Word tells us that it is still possible for you to be saved in spite of it all.

In Revelation chapter 7 there are two different groups of "saints" mentioned. In the first part of the chapter you will see a group of 144,000 saints who represent a godly remnant from the nation of Israel. There are 12,000 saints from each of the 12 tribes belonging to Israel (Revelation 7:4-8). You may already be hearing of the phenomena of these 144,000. Some students of Bible prophecy on this side of the rapture speculate that they will be like 144,000 Billy Grahams running around the world! These 144,000 are marked with a seal. In Revelation 7:1-3 we read:

> And after these things I saw four angels standing on the four corners of the earth, holding the four winds of the earth, that the wind should not blow on the earth, nor on the sea, nor on any tree. And I saw another angel ascending from the east, having the seal of the living God, and he cried with a loud voice to the four angels, to whom it was given to hurt the earth and the sea, saying, Hurt not the earth, neither the sea, nor the trees, till we have sealed the servants of our God in their foreheads.

Just as the Antichrist has a mark designating his own during the tribulation period, God also has a seal to mark His own. The angels are not to judge the earth until God's children have received this seal, thereby protecting them from what is about to befall the earth.

We said earlier that there is another group of saints in Revelation chapter 7. These are Gentile saints who have come from the other nations of the world. In verses 9 and 10 we read of John's vision:

> After this I beheld, and, lo, a great multitude, which no man could number, of all nations, and kindreds, and people, and tongues, stood before the throne, and before the Lamb, clothed with white robes, and palms in their hands; and cried with a loud voice, saying, Salvation to our God which sitteth upon the throne, and unto the Lamb.

The fact that these saints are from the tribulation comes out in verses 13 and 14:

> And one of the elders answered, saying unto me, What are these which are arrayed in white robes? And whence came they? And I said unto him, Sir, thou knowest. And he said to me, These are they which came out of great tribulation, and have washed their robes, and made them white.

The white robes refer back to Revelation 6:9-11, which identifies these tribulation saints as martyrs:

> And when he had opened the fifth seal, I saw under the altar the souls of them that were slain for the word of God, and for the testimony which they held. And they cried

> with a loud voice, saying, How long, O
> Lord, holy and true, dost thou not judge
> and avenge our blood on them that dwell
> on the earth? And white robes were given
> unto every one of them; and it was said
> unto them, that they should rest yet for a
> little season, until their fellowservants also
> and their brethren, that should be killed as
> they were, should be fulfilled.

So these are saints who have come out of the tribulation, saints who have died for their faith in Jesus Christ because they refused to bow down and worship the Antichrist.

It is imperative that you become a believer in Jesus Christ if you are to spend eternity with Him. You may have to go through some horrible suffering for your faith in Jesus Christ. It may even cost you your life like the martyred saints of Revelation 6 and 7. Or you may survive in your present body until the coming of the Lord.

As we sit here and write these words for you, we feel so inadequate. I know we've said it before, but if we were to sit here right now and say to you that we had any real understanding of what you are going through, we would be lying. There is no way we can begin to imagine what the world is like that you are living in and what a terrible time it must be, but we know the God who knows. We have already met Jesus and we know that whatever trials you are going through, Jesus is greater than those trials. The apostle Paul wrote:

I know whom I have believed, and am
persuaded that he is able to keep that
which I have committed unto him against
that day (2 Timothy 1:12).

We know that God is like a covering that will sur-
round you. He can give you the strength you need to
make it through. But to receive this you have to make a
decision for Christ. You need to make the decision right
now to give your heart to Christ, and maybe even to
give your very life for Christ. But the pain and suffering only last for a season when compared to eternity.

The alternative is not pleasant, either. It may
postpone some trials, tribulations, and suffering,
but it's far worse because it lasts for eternity.
Matthew 13:42 says that God shall cast unbelievers
"into a furnace of fire; there shall be wailing and
gnashing of teeth." And Revelation 20:15 says that
whoever is not written in the "book of life" will
be cast into the "lake of fire" along with the devil,
the beast, and the false prophet where they "shall
be tormented day and night for ever and ever"
(Revelation 20:10).

Trust in God to bring you through this tribulation, even if it means becoming a martyred saint. On
the other side you will be able to sing praises to God
for your salvation. God makes a promise to all the
tribulation saints in Revelation 7:16,17:

They shall hunger no more, neither thirst
any more; neither shall the sun light on
them, nor any heat. For the Lamb which is
in the midst of the throne shall feed them,

and shall lead them unto living fountains of waters, and God shall wipe away all tears from their eyes.

How Can I Be Saved?

Now that you know it is not too late to be saved, you must be wondering *how* you can be saved. John 3:16 is a well-known Scripture. It says:

For God so loved the world, that he gave his only begotten Son, that whosoever believeth in him should not perish, but have everlasting life.

What a fantastic gift! No one has to do anything great to deserve this gift. All you have to do is believe God in the midst of whatever trials you are experiencing. Romans 10:9 says:

That if thou shalt confess with thy mouth the Lord Jesus, and shalt believe in thine heart that God hath raised him from the dead, thou shalt be saved.

First John 1:9 says:

If we confess our sins, he is faithful and just to forgive us our sins, and to cleanse us from all unrighteousness.

This is what the power of salvation is all about: confessing our sins and confessing the Lord Jesus.

Just make a decision for Jesus Christ, and God will take care of the rest, even in the midst of trouble.

If you want to spend eternity with Jesus Christ, take a moment now to say the following prayer. This prayer will set your eternal destiny and place you in heaven. But let us add something first. This is not a magic spell or incantation that will get you into heaven. The issue isn't saying the right words. What counts is that you say these words (or similar words) while believing with all of your heart and asking with all of your heart. God is not fooled by words or appearances. He knows the heart of every individual person. When you pray sincerely for forgiveness of your sins, asking Jesus Christ to become your Savior, then God will hear and receive your prayer. If this is your sincere desire, then pray:

> Dear Father in heaven, I realize that I am a sinner and worthy of the fires of hell. At this moment I confess my sins and ask You to forgive me for my rebellion against You and my refusal to accept the love of Christ. I accept the sacrifice that Your Son Jesus made for me on Calvary's cross. I believe that You raised Him from the dead. I confess with my mouth that Jesus is my Lord. Thank You for hearing this prayer and accepting me into the family of God because of the blood of Christ that covers my sins. And I know that from this moment on I am saved. Thank You, Lord.

It's that simple. There is nothing more complicated to salvation than this. All you have to do is pray with a believing heart. Before the rapture took place, we would have suggested that you start studying the Bible to get to know the God of your salvation and Jesus Christ. We would have suggested that you find a church to attend that follows the teachings of the Bible. We would have suggested that you get together with other Christians so that you could pray with one another and encourage one another. But we are sure that this is not easy (if it's even possible) during the time in which you are living.

We can't perceive what you must be going through, but we do know that God is able. He is able to make a way where there is no way. He is able to make a path in the desert. He can cause rivers to spring up where there is no water. He can lead, guide, and direct you every step of the way. Whatever your fate on this earth may be, follow Christ. We can't wait to meet you in eternity!

CHAPTER ELEVEN

IF I READ THIS BOOK BEFORE THE RAPTURE, CAN I WAIT TO BE SAVED?

When we wrote this book, we knew that there would be some of you on this side of the rapture who would read it. We knew that some readers would be Christians who would be encouraged to know that our Lord is coming soon. But we also knew that some of you would not be Christians. If you are reading this book before the rapture, and you have not yet made a decision for Jesus Christ, we want to address this chapter directly to you.

You may be thinking that you're not really quite sure if you believe what we're saying. Maybe you're not convinced that God exists. Or maybe you're just having too much fun right now, and becoming a Christian would cramp your style.

You may be sitting back right now thinking that once the rapture takes place and you begin to see things fall into place as we told you they would, then you will know for sure, so you can decide then. Maybe you're thinking that if you see things develop as we said, then you will take both Jesus Christ and becoming a Christian more seriously.

This was of great concern to us when we wrote this book. First of all, we hope that some of the things we have explained about the Antichrist and the tribulation period will be enough to convince you that you don't want to be around then.

The tribulation will not be fun. If you're one who doesn't want to be a Christian right now because it will spoil your fun, all your good times will soon be forgotten once the tribulation is in effect. The tribulation is the most wicked of all eras in history. It will be a time of great suffering for all mankind—not just those who decide to accept Jesus Christ as their Lord and refuse to bow down to the Antichrist.

Revelation 16 says that those who take the mark of the beast will suffer from grievous sores. The sea will become as blood, and all living things in the sea will die. The rivers will be turned to blood. Men will be scorched with great heat and will suffer from plagues. What starts as a time of peace and promise will quickly turn into a time of war and judgment as God truly lets man have his own way.

We sincerely pray that you can see the seriousness of this and make a decision for Christ right now. We hope that your pride won't stop you. We hope that you will not be a part of that last-day Battle at Armageddon, so full of arrogance that you think you can make war with God and win.

This, however, was only part of our concern about you reading this book before the rapture. We were also concerned that you would think that if you decided to gamble and wait, you can still be saved after the rapture. After all, we told you that people will be saved during the tribulation.

We have to warn you about this. If you openly and willfully reject Jesus Christ right now as your Savior, we don't necessarily believe that you will have another chance on the other side. We doubt whether you will have the option of becoming one of the tribulation saints afterward.

God's Word says that those who reject Jesus Christ right now *will* believe a lie after the rapture takes place. In 2 Thessalonians 2:6-12 you can read for yourself that this is so:

> And now ye know what withholdeth that he might be revealed in his time. For the mystery of iniquity doth already work; only he who now letteth will let, until he be taken out of the way. And then shall that Wicked be revealed, whom the Lord shall consume with the spirit of his mouth, and shall destroy with the brightness of his coming, even him, whose coming is after the working of Satan with all power and signs and lying wonders, and with all deceivableness of unrighteousness in them that perish; because they received not the love of the truth, that they might be saved. And for this

cause, God shall send them strong delusion, that they should believe a lie, that they all might be damned who believed not the truth, but had pleasure in unrighteousness.

If you refuse to become a Christian now for whatever reason, God's Word says that you will be deluded and will believe all the lies of the Antichrist and the false prophet on the other side. There is no second chance. We believe that those who become saints during the tribulation are those who have never heard or fully understood the gospel of Jesus Christ.

Today Is the Day

Today each of us faces his or her own personal Armageddon. We must choose which side we will be on. Those who reject God will grow closer and closer to a very subtle but real decision to join forces with the spirit of Antichrist, blaspheme God, and fight against Christ in this hopeless battle. You are already on one of two roads. There is no other option.

According to opinion polls, an overwhelming majority of North Americans believe they will spend eternity in heaven (about 93 to 95 percent). Yet it is obvious from the moral decay and decadence that such a majority does not really have the love of Christ in its heart.

Many of these people who believe they are going to heaven apparently think they deserve to go because they were born in "Christian" nations or because their families have weddings and funerals in "Christian" churches or because their ancestors were members of such churches. But none of these credentials will get anyone into heaven.

Others point out that they are good people. They don't kick their neighbor's cat or cheat too much on their taxes. But none of these things have any bearing on a person's eternal destiny. The Bible tells us very clearly in the book of Romans that "all have sinned, and come short of the glory of God" (Romans 3:23). John tells us that if any man says he has not sinned, he is a liar (1 John 1:8,10).

No matter how good a person you are, you are still a sinner in the righteous eyes of God. You can never be good enough to be in His presence.

Imagine you were a great high jumper. You could have won an Olympic medal in that event. But no matter how talented you were, you couldn't jump to the moon. That is a picture of how close our efforts at reaching God with our good works come. No one can do it. But, thank God, we don't have to!

The Price Has Been Paid

God knew you couldn't make it. The entire Old Testament law was simply proof of how good you would have to be to make it to God by your own merits. The gulf of sin that separates us from God is just too great for us to cross.

That's why God has paid the price for us. God sent His only begotten Son, Jesus, to pay the penalty for the sins of all mankind. Jesus, who knew no sin, became our sin offering. He offered His own life to God as the payment for our sins. He agreed to suffer the agony and indignity of Calvary's cruel cross to enable you and me to avoid eternal punishment and enjoy eternal life with Him:

> For God so loved the world [mankind], that he gave his only begotten Son, that whosoever believeth in him should not perish, but have everlasting life (John 3:16).

Jesus died for the sins of all mankind. You have only to realize that you are a sinner and need a Savior, and then accept the sacrifice that Jesus made for you. Those who have done that are the "redeemed" of the Lord. Jesus, by His shed blood, has redeemed us, purchased us, bought us back for the Father. Because we have been reconciled to God, we are His children by adoption.

Right now, as you are reading this book, you can become one of the redeemed of the Lord. If you will admit you are a sinner, confess your sins, and ask God to forgive you based on the fact that Jesus has already paid the penalty for your sins, then God will forgive you. "If we confess our sins, he is faithful and just to forgive us" (1 John 1:9). The blood of Jesus cleanses us from all unrighteousness. Your sins will be washed away by the blood of Christ.

Salvation is God's free gift. Forgiveness of sins is granted on the basis of God's grace and mercy. We can't earn forgiveness. There are no good works that can save us. Yet today you can know forgiveness for your sins and freedom in Christ Jesus.

Why Not Come Home?

If this is your desire, pray the following prayer and be totally honest and sincere with God:

> Dear Father in heaven, I realize that I am a sinner and worthy of the fires of hell. At this moment I confess my sins and ask You to forgive me for my rebellion against You and my refusal to accept the love of Christ. I accept the sacrifice that Your Son Jesus made for me on Calvary's cross. I believe that You raised Him from the dead. I confess with my mouth that Jesus is my Lord. Thank You for hearing this prayer and accepting me into the family of God because of the blood of Christ that covers my sins. And I know that from this moment on I am saved. Thank You, Lord.

These are simple words. There is nothing complicated about the gospel. In fact, the Bible tells us that the way is so simple that "wayfaring men, though fools [need] not err therein" (Isaiah 35:8). It isn't hard to understand the gospel. Nothing could be clearer:

> That if thou shalt confess with thy mouth the Lord Jesus, and shalt believe in thine heart that God hath raised him from the dead, thou shalt be saved (Romans 10:9).

But there is a wise saying to the effect that knowing what to do is not the problem; doing what we know, is. It is just as true in the spiritual world. The Lord may have been dealing with you for a long time. But, like those poor souls at the Battle of Armageddon, you have chosen to make war with the Lord instead of bowing before Him.

The hard part is not saying the words; it is saying them with all of your heart. But do not fear, "For it is God which worketh in you both to will and to do of his good pleasure" (Philippians 2:13). God is for you. He is drawing you to Him by His Spirit. He has a plan for you.

But you must decide. Choose this day whom you will serve.

The Bible tells us that the angels rejoice each time a sinner comes to Christ. We rejoice with you now if you have made this most important decision in your life. We can only say, "Welcome home!"

> We then, as workers together with him, beseech you also that ye receive not the grace of God in vain. (For he saith, I have heard thee in a time accepted, and in the day of salvation have I succoured thee: behold, now is the accepted time; behold, now is the day of salvation) (2 Corinthians 6:1,2).

Appendix

Matthew

Chapter 24

1 And Jesus went out, and departed from the temple: and his disciples came to him for to shew him the buildings of the temple.

2 And Jesus said unto them, See ye not all these things? verily I say unto you, There shall not be left here one stone upon another, that shall not be thrown down.

3 And as he sat upon the mount of Olives, the disciples came unto him privately, saying, Tell us, when shall these things be? and what shall be the sign of thy coming, and of the end of the world?

4 And Jesus answered and said unto them, Take heed that no man deceive you.

5 For many shall come in my name, saying, I am Christ; and shall deceive many.

6 And ye shall hear of wars and rumours of wars: see that ye be not troubled: for all these things must come to pass, but the end is not yet.

7 For nation shall rise against nation, and kingdom against kingdom: and there shall be famines, and pestilences, and earthquakes, in divers places.

8 All these are the beginning of sorrows.

9 Then shall they deliver you up to be afflicted, and shall kill you: and ye shall be hated of all nations for my name's sake.

10 And then shall many be offended, and shall betray one another, and shall hate one another.

11 And many false prophets shall rise, and shall deceive many.

12 And because iniquity shall abound, the love of many shall wax cold.

13 But he that shall endure unto the end, the same shall be saved.

14 And this gospel of the kingdom shall be preached in all the world for a witness unto all nations; and then shall the end come.

15 When ye therefore shall see the abomination of desolation, spoken of by Daniel the prophet, stand in the holy place, (whoso readeth, let him understand:)

16 Then let them which be in Judaea flee into the mountains:

17 Let him which is on the housetop not come down to take any thing out of his house:

18 Neither let him which is in the field return back to take his clothes.

19 And woe unto them that are with child, and to them that give suck in those days!

20 But pray ye that your flight be not in the winter, neither on the sabbath day:

21 For then shall be great tribulation, such as was not since the beginning of the world to this time, no, nor ever shall be.

22 And except those days should be shortened, there should no flesh be saved: but for the elect's sake those days shall be shortened.

23 Then if any man shall say unto you, Lo, here is Christ, or there; believe it not.

24 For there shall arise false Christs, and false prophets, and shall shew great signs and wonders; insomuch that, if it were possible, they shall deceive the very elect.

25 Behold, I have told you before.

26 Wherefore if they shall say unto you, Behold, he is in the desert; go not forth: behold, he is in the secret chambers; believe it not.

27 For as the lightning cometh out of the east, and shineth even unto the west; so shall also the coming of the Son of man be.

28 For wheresoever the carcase is, there will the eagles be gathered together.

29 Immediately after the tribulation of those days shall the sun be darkened, and the moon shall not give her light, and the stars shall fall from heaven, and the powers of the heavens shall be shaken:

30 And then shall appear the sign of the Son of man in heaven: and then shall all the tribes of the earth mourn, and they shall see the Son of man coming in the clouds of heaven with power and great glory.

31 And he shall send his angels with a great sound of a trumpet, and they shall gather together his elect from the four winds, from one end of heaven to the other.

32 Now learn a parable of the fig tree; When his branch is yet tender, and putteth forth leaves, ye know that summer is nigh:

33 So likewise ye, when ye shall see all these things, know that it is near, even at the doors.

34 Verily I say unto you, This generation shall not pass, till all these things be fulfilled.

35 Heaven and earth shall pass away, but my words shall not pass away.

36 But of that day and hour knoweth no man, no, not the angels of heaven, but my Father only.

37 But as the days of Noe were, so shall also the coming of the Son of man be.

38 For as in the days that were before the flood they were eating and drinking, marrying and giving in marriage, until the day that Noe entered into the ark,

39 And knew not until the flood came, and took them all away; so shall also the coming of the Son of man be.

40 Then shall two be in the field; the one shall be taken, and the other left.

41 Two women shall be grinding at the mill; the one shall be taken, and the other left.

42 Watch therefore: for ye know not what hour your lord doth come.

43 But know this, that if the goodman of the house had known in what watch the thief would come, he would have watched, and would not have suffered his house to be broken up.

44 Therefore be ye also ready: for in such an hour as ye think not the Son of man cometh.

45 Who then is a faithful and wise servant, whom his lord hath made ruler over his household, to give them meat in due season?

46 Blessed is that servant, whom his lord when he cometh shall find so doing.

47 Verily I say unto you, That he shall make him ruler over all his goods.

48 But and if that evil servant shall say in his heart, My lord delayeth his coming;

49 And shall begin to smite his fellowservants, and to eat and drink with the drunken;

50 The lord of that servant shall come in a day when he looketh not for him, and in an hour that he is not aware of,

51 And shall cut him asunder, and appoint him his portion with the hypocrites: there shall be weeping and gnashing of teeth.

Ezekiel

Chapter 37

1 The hand of the LORD was upon me, and carried me out in the spirit of the LORD, and set me down in the midst of the valley which was full of bones,

2 And caused me to pass by them round about: and, behold, there were very many in the open valley; and, lo, they were very dry.

3 And he said unto me, Son of man, can these bones live? And I answered, O Lord GOD, thou knowest.

4 Again he said unto me, Prophesy upon these bones, and say unto them, O ye dry bones, hear the word of the LORD.

5 Thus saith the Lord GOD unto these bones; Behold, I will cause breath to enter into you, and ye shall live:

6 And I will lay sinews upon you, and will bring up flesh upon you, and cover you with skin, and put breath in you, and ye shall live; and ye shall know that I am the LORD.

7 So I prophesied as I was commanded: and as I prophesied, there was a noise, and behold a shaking, and the bones came together, bone to his bone.

8 And when I beheld, lo, the sinews and the flesh came up upon them, and the skin covered them above: but there was no breath in them.

9 Then said he unto me, Prophesy unto the wind, prophesy, son of man, and say to the wind, Thus saith the Lord GOD; Come from the four winds, O breath, and breathe upon these slain, that they may live.

10 So I prophesied as he commanded me, and the breath came into them, and they lived, and stood up upon their feet, an exceeding great army.

11 Then he said unto me, Son of man, these bones are the whole house of Israel: behold, they say, Our bones are dried, and our hope is lost: we are cut off for our parts.

12 Therefore prophesy and say unto them, Thus saith the Lord GOD; Behold, O my people, I will open your graves, and cause you to come up out of your graves, and bring you into the land of Israel.

13 And ye shall know that I am the LORD, when I have opened your graves, O my people, and brought you up out of your graves,

14 And shall put my spirit in you, and ye shall live, and I shall place you in your own land: then shall ye know that I the LORD have spoken it, and performed it, saith the LORD.

15 The word of the LORD came again unto me, saying,

16 Moreover, thou son of man, take thee one stick, and write upon it, For Judah, and for the children of Israel his companions: then take another stick, and write upon it, For Joseph, the stick of Ephraim, and for all the house of Israel his companions:

17 And join them one to another into one stick; and they shall become one in thine hand.

18 And when the children of thy people shall speak unto thee, saying, Wilt thou not shew us what thou meanest by these?

19 Say unto them, Thus saith the Lord GOD; Behold, I will take the stick of Joseph, which is in the hand of Ephraim, and the tribes of Israel his fellows, and will put them with him, even with the stick of Judah, and make them one stick, and they shall be one in mine hand.

20 And the sticks whereon thou writest shall be in thine hand before their eyes.

21 And say unto them, Thus saith the Lord GOD; Behold, I will take the children of Israel from among the heathen, whither they be gone, and will gather them on every side, and bring them into their own land:

22 And I will make them one nation in the land upon the mountains of Israel; and one king shall be king to them all: and they shall be no more two nations, neither shall they be divided into two kingdoms any more at all:

23 Neither shall they defile themselves any more with their idols, nor with their detestable things, nor with any of their transgressions: but I will save them out of all their dwellingplaces, wherein they have sinned, and will cleanse them: so shall they be my people, and I will be their God.

24 And David my servant shall be king over them; and they all shall have one shepherd: they shall also walk in my judgments, and observe my statutes, and do them.

25 And they shall dwell in the land that I have given unto Jacob my servant, wherein your fathers have dwelt; and they shall dwell therein, even they, and their children, and their children's children for ever: and my servant David shall be their prince for ever.

26 Moreover I will make a covenant of peace with them; it shall be an everlasting covenant with them: and I will place them, and multiply them, and will set my sanctuary in the midst of them for evermore.

27 My tabernacle also shall be with them: yea, I will be their God, and they shall be my people.

28 And the heathen shall know that I the Lord do sanctify Israel, when my sanctuary shall be in the midst of them for evermore.

Ezekiel

Chapter 38

1 And the word of the Lord came unto me, saying,

2 Son of man, set thy face against Gog, the land of Magog, the chief prince of Meshech and Tubal, and prophesy against him,

3 And say, Thus saith the Lord God; Behold, I am against thee, O Gog, the chief prince of Meshech and Tubal:

4 And I will turn thee back, and put hooks into thy jaws, and I will bring thee forth, and all thine army, horses and horsemen, all of them clothed with all sorts of armour, even a great company with bucklers and shields, all of them handling swords:

5 Persia, Ethiopia, and Libya with them; all of them with shield and helmet:

6 Gomer, and all his bands; the house of Togarmah of the north quarters, and all his bands: and many people with thee.

7 Be thou prepared, and prepare for thyself, thou, and all thy company that are assembled unto thee, and be thou a guard unto them.

8 After many days thou shalt be visited: in the latter years thou shalt come into the land that is brought back from the sword, and is gathered out of many people, against the mountains of Israel, which have been always waste: but it is brought forth out of the nations, and they shall dwell safely all of them.

9 Thou shalt ascend and come like a storm, thou shalt be like a cloud to cover the land, thou, and all thy bands, and many people with thee.

10 Thus saith the Lord God; It shall also come to pass, that at the same time shall things come into thy mind, and thou shalt think an evil thought:

11 And thou shalt say, I will go up to the land of unwalled villages; I will go to them that are at rest, that dwell safely, all of them dwelling without walls, and having neither bars nor gates,

12 To take a spoil, and to take a prey; to turn thine hand upon the desolate places that are now inhabited, and upon the people that are gathered out of the nations, which have gotten cattle and goods, that dwell in the midst of the land.

13 Sheba, and Dedan, and the merchants of Tarshish, with all the young lions thereof, shall say unto thee, Art thou come to take a spoil? hast thou gathered thy company to take a prey? to carry away silver and gold, to take away cattle and goods, to take a great spoil?

14 Therefore, son of man, prophesy and say unto Gog, Thus saith the Lord GOD; In that day when my people of Israel dwelleth safely, shalt thou not know it?

15 And thou shalt come from thy place out of the north parts, thou, and many people with thee, all of them riding upon horses, a great company, and a mighty army:

16 And thou shalt come up against my people of Israel, as a cloud to cover the land; it shall be in the latter days, and I will bring thee against my land, that the heathen may know me, when I shall be sanctified in thee, O Gog, before their eyes.

17 Thus saith the Lord GOD; Art thou he of whom I have spoken in old time by my servants the prophets of Israel, which prophesied in those days many years that I would bring thee against them?

18 And it shall come to pass at the same time when Gog shall come against the land of Israel, saith the Lord GOD, that my fury shall come up in my face.

19 For in my jealousy and in the fire of my wrath have I spoken, Surely in that day there shall be a great shaking in the land of Israel;

20 So that the fishes of the sea, and the fowls of the heaven, and the beasts of the field, and all creeping things that creep upon the earth, and all the men that are upon the face of the earth, shall shake at my presence, and the mountains shall be thrown down, and the steep places shall fall, and every wall shall fall to the ground.

21 And I will call for a sword against him throughout all my mountains, saith the Lord GOD: every man's sword shall be against his brother.

22 And I will plead against him with pestilence and with blood; and I will rain upon him, and upon his bands, and upon the many people that are with him, an overflowing rain, and great hailstones, fire, and brimstone.

23 Thus will I magnify myself, and sanctify myself; and I will be known in the eyes of many nations, and they shall know that I am the LORD.

Ezekiel

Chapter 39

1 Therefore, thou son of man, prophesy against Gog, and say, Thus saith the Lord GOD; Behold, I am against thee, O Gog, the chief prince of Meshech and Tubal:

2 And I will turn thee back, and leave but the sixth part of thee, and will cause thee to come up from the north parts, and will bring thee upon the mountains of Israel:

3 And I will smite thy bow out of thy left hand, and will cause thine arrows to fall out of thy right hand.

4 Thou shalt fall upon the mountains of Israel, thou, and all thy bands, and the people that is with thee: I will give thee unto the ravenous birds of every sort, and to the beasts of the field to be devoured.

5 Thou shalt fall upon the open field: for I have spoken it, saith the Lord GOD.

6 And I will send a fire on Magog, and among them that dwell carelessly in the isles: and they shall know that I am the LORD.

7 So will I make my holy name known in the midst of my people Israel; and I will not let them pollute my holy name any more: and the heathen shall know that I am the LORD, the Holy One in Israel.

8 Behold, it is come, and it is done, saith the Lord GOD; this is the day whereof I have spoken.

9 And they that dwell in the cities of Israel shall go forth, and shall set on fire and burn the weapons, both the shields and the bucklers, the bows and the arrows, and the handstaves, and the spears, and they shall burn them with fire seven years:

10 So that they shall take no wood out of the field, neither cut down any out of the forests; for they shall burn the weapons with fire: and they shall spoil those that spoiled them, and rob those that robbed them, saith the Lord GOD.

11 And it shall come to pass in that day, that I will give unto Gog a place there of graves in Israel, the valley of the passengers on the east of the sea: and it shall stop the noses of the passengers: and there shall they bury Gog and all his multitude: and they shall call it The valley of Hamon-gog.

12 And seven months shall the house of Israel be burying of them, that they may cleanse the land.

13 Yea, all the people of the land shall bury them; and it shall be to them a renown the day that I shall be glorified, saith the Lord GOD.

14 And they shall sever out men of continual employment, passing through the land to bury with the passengers those that remain upon the face of the earth, to cleanse it: after the end of seven months shall they search.

15 And the passengers that pass through the land, when any seeth a man's bone, then shall he set up a sign by it, till the buriers have buried it in the valley of Hamon-gog.

16 And also the name of the city shall be Hamonah. Thus shall they cleanse the land.

17 And, thou son of man, thus saith the Lord GOD; Speak unto every feathered fowl, and to every beast of the field, Assemble yourselves, and come; gather yourselves on every side to my sacrifice that I do sacrifice for you, even a great sacrifice upon the mountains of Israel, that ye may eat flesh, and drink blood.

18 Ye shall eat the flesh of the mighty, and drink the blood of the princes of the earth, of rams, of lambs, and of goats, of bullocks, all of them fatlings of Bashan.

19 And ye shall eat fat till ye be full, and drink blood till ye be drunken, of my sacrifice which I have sacrificed for you.

20 Thus ye shall be filled at my table with horses and chariots, with mighty men, and with all men of war, saith the Lord GOD.

21 And I will set my glory among the heathen, and all the heathen shall see my judgment that I have executed, and my hand that I have laid upon them.

22 So the house of Israel shall know that I am the LORD their God from that day and forward.

23 And the heathen shall know that the house of Israel went into captivity for their iniquity: because they trespassed against me, therefore hid I my face from them, and gave them into the hand of their enemies: so fell they all by the sword.

24 According to their uncleanness and according to their transgressions have I done unto them, and hid my face from them.

25 Therefore thus saith the Lord GOD; Now will I bring again the captivity of Jacob, and have mercy upon the whole house of Israel, and will be jealous for my holy name;

26 After that they have borne their shame, and all their trespasses whereby they have trespassed against me, when they dwelt safely in their land, and none made them afraid.

27 When I have brought them again from the people, and gathered them out of their enemies' lands, and am sanctified in them in the sight of many nations;

28 Then shall they know that I am the LORD their God, which caused them to be led into captivity among the heathen: but I have gathered them unto their own land, and have left none of them any more there.

29 Neither will I hide my face any more from them: for I have poured out my spirit upon the house of Israel, saith the Lord GOD.

Daniel

Chapter 7

1 In the first year of Belshazzar king of Babylon Daniel had a dream and visions of his head upon his bed: then he wrote the dream, and told the sum of the matters.

2 Daniel spake and said, I saw in my vision by night, and, behold, the four winds of the heaven strove upon the great sea.

3 And four great beasts came up from the sea, diverse one from another.

4 The first was like a lion, and had eagle's wings: I beheld till the wings thereof were plucked, and it was lifted up from the earth, and made stand upon the feet as a man, and a man's heart was given to it.

5 And behold another beast, a second, like to a bear, and it raised up itself on one side, and it had three ribs in the mouth of it between the teeth of it: and they said thus unto it, Arise, devour much flesh.

6 After this I beheld, and lo another, like a leopard, which had upon the back of it four wings of a fowl; the beast had also four heads; and dominion was given to it.

7 After this I saw in the night visions, and behold a fourth beast, dreadful and terrible, and strong exceedingly; and it had great iron teeth: it devoured and brake in pieces, and stamped the residue with the feet of it: and it was diverse from all the beasts that were before it; and it had ten horns.

8 I considered the horns, and, behold, there came up among them another little horn, before whom there were three of the first horns plucked up by the roots: and, behold, in this horn were eyes like the eyes of man, and a mouth speaking great things.

9 I beheld till the thrones were cast down, and the Ancient of days did sit, whose garment was white as snow, and the hair of his head like the pure wool: his throne was like the fiery flame, and his wheels as burning fire.

10 A fiery stream issued and came forth from before him: thousand thousands ministered unto him, and ten thousand times ten thousand stood before him: the judgment was set, and the books were opened.

11 I beheld then because of the voice of the great words which the horn spake: I beheld even till the beast was slain, and his body destroyed, and given to the burning flame.

12 As concerning the rest of the beasts, they had their dominion taken away: yet their lives were prolonged for a season and time.

13 I saw in the night visions, and, behold, one like the Son of man came with the clouds of heaven, and came to the Ancient of days, and they brought him near before him.

14 And there was given him dominion, and glory, and a kingdom, that all people, nations, and languages, should serve him: his dominion is an everlasting dominion, which shall not pass away, and his kingdom that which shall not be destroyed.

15 I Daniel was grieved in my spirit in the midst of my body, and the visions of my head troubled me.

16 I came near unto one of them that stood by, and asked him the truth of all this. So he told me, and made me know the interpretation of the things.

17 These great beasts, which are four, are four kings, which shall arise out of the earth.

18 But the saints of the most High shall take the kingdom, and possess the kingdom for ever, even for ever and ever.

19 Then I would know the truth of the fourth beast, which was diverse from all the others, exceeding dreadful, whose teeth were of iron, and his nails of brass; which devoured, brake in pieces, and stamped the residue with his feet;

20 And of the ten horns that were in his head, and of the other which came up, and before whom three fell; even of that horn that had eyes, and a mouth that spake very great things, whose look was more stout than his fellows.

21 I beheld, and the same horn made war with the saints, and prevailed against them;

22 Until the Ancient of days came, and judgment was given to the saints of the most High; and the time came that the saints possessed the kingdom.

23 Thus he said, The fourth beast shall be the fourth kingdom upon earth, which shall be diverse from all kingdoms, and shall devour the whole earth, and shall tread it down, and break it in pieces.

24 And the ten horns out of this kingdom are ten kings that shall arise: and another shall rise after them; and he shall be diverse from the first, and he shall subdue three kings.

25 And he shall speak great words against the most High, and shall wear out the saints of the most High, and think to change times and laws: and they shall be given into his hand until a time and times and the dividing of time.

26 But the judgment shall sit, and they shall take away his dominion, to consume and to destroy it unto the end.

27 And the kingdom and dominion, and the greatness of the kingdom under the whole heaven, shall be given to the people of the saints of the most High, whose kingdom is an everlasting kingdom, and all dominions shall serve and obey him.

28 Hitherto is the end of the matter. As for me Daniel, my cogitations much troubled me, and my countenance changed in me: but I kept the matter in my heart.

The Book of Revelation

Chapter 1

1 The Revelation of Jesus Christ, which God gave unto him, to shew unto his servants things which must shortly come to pass; and he sent and signified it by his angel unto his servant John:

2 Who bare record of the word of God, and of the testimony of Jesus Christ, and of all things that he saw.

3 Blessed is he that readeth, and they that hear the words of this prophecy, and keep those things which are written therein: for the time is at hand.

4 John to the seven churches which are in Asia: Grace be unto you, and peace, from him which is, and which was, and which is to come; and from the seven Spirits which are before his throne;

5 And from Jesus Christ, who is the faithful witness, and the first begotten of the dead, and the prince of the kings of the earth. Unto him that loved us, and washed us from our sins in his own blood,

6 And hath made us kings and priests unto God and his Father; to him be glory and dominion for ever and ever. Amen.

7 Behold, he cometh with clouds; and every eye shall see him, and they also which pierced him: and all kindreds of the earth shall wail because of him. Even so, Amen.

8 I am Alpha and Omega, the beginning and the ending, saith the Lord, which is, and which was, and which is to come, the Almighty.

9 I John, who also am your brother, and companion in tribulation, and in the kingdom and patience of Jesus Christ, was in the isle that is called Patmos, for the word of God, and for the testimony of Jesus Christ.

10 I was in the Spirit on the Lord's day, and heard behind me a great voice, as of a trumpet,

11 Saying, I am Alpha and Omega, the first and the last: and, What thou seest, write in a book, and send it unto the seven churches which are in Asia; unto Ephesus, and unto Smyrna, and unto Pergamos, and unto Thyatira, and unto Sardis, and unto Philadelphia, and unto Laodicea.

12 And I turned to see the voice that spake with me. And being turned, I saw seven golden candlesticks;

13 And in the midst of the seven candlesticks one like unto the Son of man, clothed with a garment down to the foot, and girt about the paps with a golden girdle.

14 His head and his hairs were white like wool, as white as snow; and his eyes were as a flame of fire;

15 And his feet like unto fine brass, as if they burned in a furnace; and his voice as the sound of many waters.

16 And he had in his right hand seven stars: and out of his mouth went a sharp twoedged sword: and his countenance was as the sun shineth in his strength.

17 And when I saw him, I fell at his feet as dead. And he laid his right hand upon me, saying unto me, Fear not; I am the first and the last:

18 I am he that liveth, and was dead; and, behold, I am alive for evermore, Amen; and have the keys of hell and of death.

19 Write the things which thou hast seen, and the things which are, and the things which shall be hereafter;

20 The mystery of the seven stars which thou sawest in my right hand, and the seven golden candlesticks. The seven stars are the angels of the seven churches: and the seven candlesticks which thou sawest are the seven churches.

Chapter 2

1 Unto the angel of the church of Ephesus write; These things saith he that holdeth the seven stars in his right hand, who walketh in the midst of the seven golden candlesticks;

2 I know thy works, and thy labour, and thy patience, and how thou canst not bear them which are evil: and thou hast tried them which say they are apostles, and are not, and hast found them liars:

3 And hast borne, and hast patience, and for my name's sake hast laboured, and hast not fainted.

4 Nevertheless I have somewhat against thee, because thou hast left thy first love.

5 Remember therefore from whence thou art fallen, and repent, and do the first works; or else I will come unto thee quickly, and will remove thy candlestick out of his place, except thou repent.

6 But this thou hast, that thou hatest the deeds of the Nicolaitans, which I also hate.

7 He that hath an ear, let him hear what the Spirit saith unto the churches; To him that overcometh will I give to eat of the tree of life, which is in the midst of the paradise of God.

8 And unto the angel of the church in Smyrna write; These things saith the first and the last, which was dead, and is alive;

9 I know thy works, and tribulation, and poverty, (but thou art rich) and I know the blasphemy of them which say they are Jews, and are not, but are the synagogue of Satan.

10 Fear none of those things which thou shalt suffer: behold, the devil shall cast some of you into prison, that ye may be tried; and ye shall have tribulation ten days: be thou faithful unto death, and I will give thee a crown of life.

11 He that hath an ear, let him hear what the Spirit saith unto the churches; He that overcometh shall not be hurt of the second death.

12 And to the angel of the church in Pergamos write; These things saith he which hath the sharp sword with two edges;

13 I know thy works, and where thou dwellest, even where Satan's seat is: and thou holdest fast my name, and hast not denied my faith, even in those days wherein Antipas was my faithful martyr, who was slain among you, where Satan dwelleth.

14 But I have a few things against thee, because thou hast there them that hold the doctrine of Balaam, who taught Balac to cast a stumblingblock before the children of Israel, to eat things sacrificed unto idols, and to commit fornication.

15 So hast thou also them that hold the doctrine of the Nicolaitans, which thing I hate.

16 Repent; or else I will come unto thee quickly, and will fight against them with the sword of my mouth.

17 He that hath an ear, let him hear what the Spirit saith unto the churches; To him that overcometh will I give to eat of the hidden manna, and will give him a white stone, and in the stone a new name written, which no man knoweth saving he that receiveth it.

18 And unto the angel of the church in Thyatira write; These things saith the Son of God, who hath his eyes like unto a flame of fire, and his feet are like fine brass;

19 I know thy works, and charity, and service, and faith, and thy patience, and thy works; and the last to be more than the first.

20 Notwithstanding I have a few things against thee, because thou sufferest that woman Jezebel, which calleth herself a prophetess, to teach and to seduce my servants to commit fornication, and to eat things sacrificed unto idols.

21 And I gave her space to repent of her fornication; and she repented not.

22 Behold, I will cast her into a bed, and them that commit adultery with her into great tribulation, except they repent of their deeds.

23 And I will kill her children with death; and all the churches shall know that I am he which searcheth the reins and hearts: and I will give unto every one of you according to your works.

24 But unto you I say, and unto the rest in Thyatira, as many as have not this doctrine, and which have not known the depths of Satan, as they speak; I will put upon you none other burden.

25 But that which ye have already hold fast till I come.

26 And he that overcometh, and keepeth my works unto the end, to him will I give power over the nations:

27 And he shall rule them with a rod of iron; as the vessels of a potter shall they be broken to shivers: even as I received of my Father.

28 And I will give him the morning star.

29 He that hath an ear, let him hear what the Spirit saith unto the churches.

Chapter 3

1 And unto the angel of the church in Sardis write; These things saith he that hath the seven Spirits of God, and the seven stars; I know thy works, that thou hast a name that thou livest, and art dead.

2 Be watchful, and strengthen the things which remain, that are ready to die: for I have not found thy works perfect before God.

3 Remember therefore how thou hast received and heard, and hold fast, and repent. If therefore thou shalt not watch, I will come on thee as a thief, and thou shalt not know what hour I will come upon thee.

4 Thou hast a few names even in Sardis which have not defiled their garments; and they shall walk with me in white: for they are worthy.

5 He that overcometh, the same shall be clothed in white raiment; and I will not blot out his name out of the book of life, but I will confess his name before my Father, and before his angels.

6 He that hath an ear, let him hear what the Spirit saith unto the churches.

7 And to the angel of the church in Philadelphia write; These things saith he that is holy, he that is true, he that hath the key of David, he that openeth, and no man shutteth; and shutteth, and no man openeth;

8 I know thy works: behold, I have set before thee an open door, and no man can shut it: for thou hast a little strength, and hast kept my word, and hast not denied my name.

9 Behold, I will make them of the synagogue of Satan, which say they are Jews, and are not, but do lie; behold, I will make them to come and worship before thy feet, and to know that I have loved thee.

10 Because thou hast kept the word of my patience, I also will keep thee from the hour of temptation, which shall come upon all the world, to try them that dwell upon the earth.

11 Behold, I come quickly: hold that fast which thou hast, that no man take thy crown.

12 Him that overcometh will I make a pillar in the temple of my God, and he shall go no more out: and I will write upon him the name of my God, and the name of the city of my God, which is new Jerusalem, which cometh down out of heaven from my God: and I will write upon him my new name.

13 He that hath an ear, let him hear what the Spirit saith unto the churches.

14 And unto the angel of the church of the Laodiceans write; These things saith the Amen, the faithful and true witness, the beginning of the creation of God;

15 I know thy works, that thou art neither cold nor hot: I would thou wert cold or hot.

16 So then because thou art lukewarm, and neither cold nor hot, I will spue thee out of my mouth.

17 Because thou sayest, I am rich, and increased with goods, and have need of nothing; and knowest not that thou art wretched, and miserable, and poor, and blind, and naked:

18 I counsel thee to buy of me gold tried in the fire, that thou mayest be rich; and white raiment, that thou mayest be clothed, and that the shame of thy nakedness do not appear; and anoint thine eyes with eyesalve, that thou mayest see.

19 As many as I love, I rebuke and chasten: be zealous therefore, and repent.

20 Behold, I stand at the door, and knock: if any man hear my voice, and open the door, I will come in to him, and will sup with him, and he with me.

21 To him that overcometh will I grant to sit with me in my throne, even as I also overcame, and am set down with my Father in his throne.

22 He that hath an ear, let him hear what the Spirit saith unto the churches.

Chapter 4

1 After this I looked, and, behold, a door was opened in heaven: and the first voice which I heard was as it were of a trumpet talking with me; which said, Come up hither, and I will shew thee things which must be hereafter.

2 And immediately I was in the spirit: and, behold, a throne was set in heaven, and one sat on the throne.

3 And he that sat was to look upon like a jasper and a sardine stone: and there was a rainbow round about the throne, in sight like unto an emerald.

4 And round about the throne were four and twenty seats: and upon the seats I saw four and twenty elders sitting, clothed in white raiment; and they had on their heads crowns of gold.

5 And out of the throne proceeded lightnings and thunderings and voices: and there were seven lamps of fire burning before the throne, which are the seven Spirits of God.

6 And before the throne there was a sea of glass like unto crystal: and in the midst of the throne, and round about the throne, were four beasts full of eyes before and behind.

7 And the first beast was like a lion, and the second beast like a calf, and the third beast had a face as a man, and the fourth beast was like a flying eagle.

8 And the four beasts had each of them six wings about him; and they were full of eyes within: and they rest not day and night, saying, Holy, holy, holy, Lord God Almighty, which was, and is, and is to come.

9 And when those beasts give glory and honour and thanks to him that sat on the throne, who liveth for ever and ever,

10 The four and twenty elders fall down before him that sat on the throne, and worship him that liveth for ever and ever, and cast their crowns before the throne, saying,

11 Thou art worthy, O Lord, to receive glory and honour and power: for thou hast created all things, and for thy pleasure they are and were created.

Chapter 5

1 And I saw in the right hand of him that sat on the throne a book written within and on the backside, sealed with seven seals.

2 And I saw a strong angel proclaiming with a loud voice, Who is worthy to open the book, and to loose the seals thereof?

3 And no man in heaven, nor in earth, neither under the earth, was able to open the book, neither to look thereon.

4 And I wept much, because no man was found worthy to open and to read the book, neither to look thereon.

5 And one of the elders saith unto me, Weep not: behold, the Lion of the tribe of Juda, the Root of David, hath prevailed to open the book, and to loose the seven seals thereof.

6 And I beheld, and, lo, in the midst of the throne and of the four beasts, and in the midst of the elders, stood a Lamb as it had been slain, having seven horns and seven eyes, which are the seven Spirits of God sent forth into all the earth.

7 And he came and took the book out of the right hand of him that sat upon the throne.

8 And when he had taken the book, the four beasts and four and twenty elders fell down before the Lamb, having every one of them harps, and golden vials full of odours, which are the prayers of saints.

9 And they sung a new song, saying, Thou art worthy to take the book, and to open the seals thereof: for thou wast slain, and hast redeemed us to God by thy blood out of every kindred, and tongue, and people, and nation;

10 And hast made us unto our God kings and priests: and we shall reign on the earth.

11 And I beheld, and I heard the voice of many angels round about the throne and the beasts and the elders: and the number of them was ten thousand times ten thousand, and thousands of thousands;

12 Saying with a loud voice, Worthy is the Lamb that was slain to receive power, and riches, and wisdom, and strength, and honour, and glory, and blessing.

13 And every creature which is in heaven, and on the earth, and under the earth, and such as are in the sea, and all that are in them, heard I saying, Blessing, and honour, and glory, and power, be unto him that sitteth upon the throne, and unto the Lamb for ever and ever.

14 And the four beasts said, Amen. And the four and twenty elders fell down and worshipped him that liveth for ever and ever.

Chapter 6

1 And I saw when the Lamb opened one of the seals, and I heard, as it were the noise of thunder, one of the four beasts saying, Come and see.

2 And I saw, and behold a white horse: and he that sat on him had a bow; and a crown was given unto him: and he went forth conquering, and to conquer.

3 And when he had opened the second seal, I heard the second beast say, Come and see.

4 And there went out another horse that was red: and power was given to him that sat thereon to take peace from the earth, and that they should kill one another: and there was given unto him a great sword.

5 And when he had opened the third seal, I heard the third beast say, Come and see. And I beheld, and lo a black horse; and he that sat on him had a pair of balances in his hand.

6 And I heard a voice in the midst of the four beasts say, A measure of wheat for a penny, and three measures of barley for a penny; and see thou hurt not the oil and the wine.

7 And when he had opened the fourth seal, I heard the voice of the fourth beast say, Come and see.

8 And I looked, and behold a pale horse: and his name that sat on him was Death, and Hell followed with him. And power was given unto them over the fourth part of the earth, to kill with sword, and with hunger, and with death, and with the beasts of the earth.

9 And when he had opened the fifth seal, I saw under the altar the souls of them that were slain for the word of God, and for the testimony which they held:

10 And they cried with a loud voice, saying, How long, O Lord, holy and true, dost thou not judge and avenge our blood on them that dwell on the earth?

11 And white robes were given unto every one of them; and it was said unto them, that they should rest yet for a little season, until their fellowservants also and their brethren, that should be killed as they were, should be fulfilled.

12 And I beheld when he had opened the sixth seal, and, lo, there was a great earthquake; and the sun became black as sackcloth of hair, and the moon became as blood;

13 And the stars of heaven fell unto the earth, even as a fig tree casteth her untimely figs, when she is shaken of a mighty wind.

14 And the heaven departed as a scroll when it is rolled together; and every mountain and island were moved out of their places.

15 And the kings of the earth, and the great men, and the rich men, and the chief captains, and the mighty men, and every bondman, and every free man, hid themselves in the dens and in the rocks of the mountains;

16 And said to the mountains and rocks, Fall on us, and hide us from the face of him that sitteth on the throne, and from the wrath of the Lamb:

17 For the great day of his wrath is come; and who shall be able to stand?

Chapter 7

1 And after these things I saw four angels standing on the four corners of the earth, holding the four winds of the earth, that the wind should not blow on the earth, nor on the sea, nor on any tree.

2 And I saw another angel ascending from the east, having the seal of the living God: and he cried with a loud voice to the four angels, to whom it was given to hurt the earth and the sea,

3 Saying, Hurt not the earth, neither the sea, nor the trees, till we have sealed the servants of our God in their foreheads.

4 And I heard the number of them which were sealed: and there were sealed an hundred and forty and four thousand of all the tribes of the children of Israel.

5 Of the tribe of Juda were sealed twelve thousand. Of the tribe of Reuben were sealed twelve thousand. Of the tribe of Gad were sealed twelve thousand.

6 Of the tribe of Aser were sealed twelve thousand. Of the tribe of Nephthalim were sealed twelve thousand. Of the tribe of Manasses were sealed twelve thousand.

7 Of the tribe of Simeon were sealed twelve thousand. Of the tribe of Levi were sealed twelve thousand. Of the tribe of Issachar were sealed twelve thousand.

8 Of the tribe of Zabulon were sealed twelve thousand. Of the tribe of Joseph were sealed twelve thousand. Of the tribe of Benjamin were sealed twelve thousand.

9 After this I beheld, and, lo, a great multitude, which no man could number, of all nations, and kindreds, and people, and tongues, stood before the throne, and before the Lamb, clothed with white robes, and palms in their hands;

10 And cried with a loud voice, saying, Salvation to our God which sitteth upon the throne, and unto the Lamb.

11 And all the angels stood round about the throne, and about the elders and the four beasts, and fell before the throne on their faces, and worshipped God,

12 Saying, Amen: Blessing, and glory, and wisdom, and thanksgiving, and honour, and power, and might, be unto our God for ever and ever. Amen.

13 And one of the elders answered, saying unto me, What are these which are arrayed in white robes? and whence came they?

14 And I said unto him, Sir, thou knowest. And he said to me, These are they which came out of great tribulation, and have washed their robes, and made them white in the blood of the Lamb.

15 Therefore are they before the throne of God, and serve him day and night in his temple: and he that sitteth on the throne shall dwell among them.

16 They shall hunger no more, neither thirst any more; neither shall the sun light on them, nor any heat.

17 For the Lamb which is in the midst of the throne shall feed them, and shall lead them unto living fountains of waters: and God shall wipe away all tears from their eyes.

Chapter 8

1 And when he had opened the seventh seal, there was silence in heaven about the space of half an hour.

2 And I saw the seven angels which stood before God; and to them were given seven trumpets.

3 And another angel came and stood at the altar, having a golden censer; and there was given unto him much incense, that he should offer it with the prayers of all saints upon the golden altar which was before the throne.

4 And the smoke of the incense, which came with the prayers of the saints, ascended up before God out of the angel's hand.

5 And the angel took the censer, and filled it with fire of the altar, and cast it into the earth: and there were voices, and thunderings, and lightnings, and an earthquake.

6 And the seven angels which had the seven trumpets prepared themselves to sound.

7 The first angel sounded, and there followed hail and fire mingled with blood, and they were cast upon the earth: and the third part of trees was burnt up, and all green grass was burnt up.

8 And the second angel sounded, and as it were a great mountain burning with fire was cast into the sea: and the third part of the sea became blood;

9 And the third part of the creatures which were in the sea, and had life, died; and the third part of the ships were destroyed.

10 And the third angel sounded, and there fell a great star from heaven, burning as it were a lamp, and it fell upon the third part of the rivers, and upon the fountains of waters;

11 And the name of the star is called Wormwood: and the third part of the waters became wormwood; and many men died of the waters, because they were made bitter.

12 And the fourth angel sounded, and the third part of the sun was smitten, and the third part of the moon, and the third part of the stars; so as the third part of them was darkened, and the day shone not for a third part of it, and the night likewise.

13 And I beheld, and heard an angel flying through the midst of heaven, saying with a loud voice, Woe, woe, woe, to the inhabiters of the earth by reason of the other voices of the trumpet of the three angels, which are yet to sound!

Chapter 9

1 And the fifth angel sounded, and I saw a star fall from heaven unto the earth: and to him was given the key of the bottomless pit.

2 And he opened the bottomless pit; and there arose a smoke out of the pit, as the smoke of a great furnace; and the sun and the air were darkened by reason of the smoke of the pit.

3 And there came out of the smoke locusts upon the earth: and unto them was given power, as the scorpions of the earth have power.

4 And it was commanded them that they should not hurt the grass of the earth, neither any green thing, neither any tree; but only those men which have not the seal of God in their foreheads.

5 And to them it was given that they should not kill them, but that they should be tormented five months: and their torment was as the torment of a scorpion, when he striketh a man.

6 And in those days shall men seek death, and shall not find it; and shall desire to die, and death shall flee from them.

7 And the shapes of the locusts were like unto horses prepared unto battle; and on their heads were as it were crowns like gold, and their faces were as the faces of men.

8 And they had hair as the hair of women, and their teeth were as the teeth of lions.

9 And they had breastplates, as it were breastplates of iron; and the sound of their wings was as the sound of chariots of many horses running to battle.

10 And they had tails like unto scorpions, and there were stings in their tails: and their power was to hurt men five months.

11 And they had a king over them, which is the angel of the bottomless pit, whose name in the Hebrew tongue is Abaddon, but in the Greek tongue hath his name Apollyon.

12 One woe is past; and, behold, there come two woes more hereafter.

13 And the sixth angel sounded, and I heard a voice from the four horns of the golden altar which is before God,

14 Saying to the sixth angel which had the trumpet, Loose the four angels which are bound in the great river Euphrates.

15 And the four angels were loosed, which were prepared for an hour, and a day, and a month, and a year, for to slay the third part of men.

16 And the number of the army of the horsemen were two hundred thousand thousand: and I heard the number of them.

17 And thus I saw the horses in the vision, and them that sat on them, having breastplates of fire, and of jacinth, and brimstone: and the heads of the horses were as the heads of lions; and out of their mouths issued fire and smoke and brimstone.

18 By these three was the third part of men killed, by the fire, and by the smoke, and by the brimstone, which issued out of their mouths.

19 For their power is in their mouth, and in their tails: for their tails were like unto serpents, and had heads, and with them they do hurt.

20 And the rest of the men which were not killed by these plagues yet repented not of the works of their hands, that they should not worship devils, and idols of gold, and silver, and brass, and stone, and of wood: which neither can see, nor hear, nor walk:

21 Neither repented they of their murders, nor of their sorceries, nor of their fornication, nor of their thefts.

Chapter 10

1 And I saw another mighty angel come down from heaven, clothed with a cloud: and a rainbow was upon his head, and his face was as it were the sun, and his feet as pillars of fire:

2 And he had in his hand a little book open: and he set his right foot upon the sea, and his left foot on the earth,

3 And cried with a loud voice, as when a lion roareth: and when he had cried, seven thunders uttered their voices.

4 And when the seven thunders had uttered their voices, I was about to write: and I heard a voice from heaven saying unto me, Seal up those things which the seven thunders uttered, and write them not.

5 And the angel which I saw stand upon the sea and upon the earth lifted up his hand to heaven,

6 And sware by him that liveth for ever and ever, who created heaven, and the things that therein are, and the earth, and the things that therein are, and the sea, and the things which are therein, that there should be time no longer:

7 But in the days of the voice of the seventh angel, when he shall begin to sound, the mystery of God should be finished, as he hath declared to his servants the prophets.

8 And the voice which I heard from heaven spake unto me again, and said, Go and take the little book which is open in the hand of the angel which standeth upon the sea and upon the earth.

9 And I went unto the angel, and said unto him, Give me the little book. And he said unto me, Take it, and eat it up; and it shall make thy belly bitter, but it shall be in thy mouth sweet as honey.

10 And I took the little book out of the angel's hand, and ate it up; and it was in my mouth sweet as honey: and as soon as I had eaten it, my belly was bitter.

11 And he said unto me, Thou must prophesy again before many peoples, and nations, and tongues, and kings.

Chapter 11

1 And there was given me a reed like unto a rod: and the angel stood, saying, Rise, and measure the temple of God, and the altar, and them that worship therein.

2 But the court which is without the temple leave out, and measure it not; for it is given unto the Gentiles: and the holy city shall they tread under foot forty and two months.

3 And I will give power unto my two witnesses, and they shall prophesy a thousand two hundred and threescore days, clothed in sackcloth.

4 These are the two olive trees, and the two candlesticks standing before the God of the earth.

5 And if any man will hurt them, fire proceedeth out of their mouth, and devoureth their enemies: and if any man will hurt them, he must in this manner be killed.

6 These have power to shut heaven, that it rain not in the days of their prophecy: and have power over waters to turn them to blood, and to smite the earth with all plagues, as often as they will.

7 And when they shall have finished their testimony, the beast that ascendeth out of the bottomless pit shall make war against them, and shall overcome them, and kill them.

8 And their dead bodies shall lie in the street of the great city, which spiritually is called Sodom and Egypt, where also our Lord was crucified.

9 And they of the people and kindreds and tongues and nations shall see their dead bodies three days and an half, and shall not suffer their dead bodies to be put in graves.

10 And they that dwell upon the earth shall rejoice over them, and make merry, and shall send gifts one to another; because these two prophets tormented them that dwelt on the earth.

11 And after three days and an half the Spirit of life from God entered into them, and they stood upon their feet; and great fear fell upon them which saw them.

12 And they heard a great voice from heaven saying unto them, Come up hither. And they ascended up to heaven in a cloud; and their enemies beheld them.

13 And the same hour was there a great earthquake, and the tenth part of the city fell, and in the earthquake were slain of men seven thousand: and the remnant were affrighted, and gave glory to the God of heaven.

14 The second woe is past; and, behold, the third woe cometh quickly.

15 And the seventh angel sounded; and there were great voices in heaven, saying, The kingdoms of this world are become the kingdoms of our Lord, and of his Christ; and he shall reign for ever and ever.

16 And the four and twenty elders, which sat before God on their seats, fell upon their faces, and worshipped God,

17 Saying, We give thee thanks, O Lord God Almighty, which art, and wast, and art to come; because thou hast taken to thee thy great power, and hast reigned.

18 And the nations were angry, and thy wrath is come, and the time of the dead, that they should be judged, and that thou shouldest give reward unto thy servants the prophets, and to the saints, and them that fear thy name, small and great; and shouldest destroy them which destroy the earth.

19 And the temple of GOD was opened in heaven, and there was seen in his temple the ark of his testament: and there were lightnings, and voices, and thunderings, and an earthquake, and great hail.

Chapter 12

1 And there appeared a great wonder in heaven; a woman clothed with the sun, and the moon under her feet, and upon her head a crown of twelve stars:

2 And she being with child cried, travailing in birth, and pained to be delivered.

3 And there appeared another wonder in heaven; and behold a great red dragon, having seven heads and ten horns, and seven crowns upon his heads.

4 And his tail drew the third part of the stars of heaven, and did cast them to the earth: and the dragon stood before the woman which was ready to be delivered, for to devour her child as soon as it was born.

5 And she brought forth a man child, who was to rule all nations with a rod of iron: and her child was caught up unto God, and to his throne.

6 And the woman fled into the wilderness, where she hath a place prepared of God, that they should feed her there a thousand two hundred and threescore days.

7 And there was war in heaven: Michael and his angels fought against the dragon; and the dragon fought and his angels,

8 And prevailed not; neither was their place found any more in heaven.

9 And the great dragon was cast out, that old serpent, called the Devil, and Satan, which deceiveth the whole world: he was cast out into the earth, and his angels were cast out with him.

10 And I heard a loud voice saying in heaven, Now is come salvation, and strength, and the kingdom of our God, and the power of his Christ: for the accuser of our brethren is cast down, which accused them before our God day and night.

11 And they overcame him by the blood of the Lamb, and by the word of their testimony; and they loved not their lives unto the death.

12 Therefore rejoice, ye heavens, and ye that dwell in them. Woe to the inhabiters of the earth and of the sea! for the devil is come down unto you, having great wrath, because he knoweth that he hath but a short time.

13 And when the dragon saw that he was cast unto the earth, he persecuted the woman which brought forth the man child.

14 And to the woman were given two wings of a great eagle, that she might fly into the wilderness, into her place, where she is nourished for a time, and times, and half a time, from the face of the serpent.

15 And the serpent cast out of his mouth water as a flood after the woman, that he might cause her to be carried away of the flood.

16 And the earth helped the woman, and the earth opened her mouth, and swallowed up the flood which the dragon cast out of his mouth.

17 And the dragon was wroth with the woman, and went to make war with the remnant of her seed, which keep the commandments of God, and have the testimony of Jesus Christ.

Chapter 13

1 And I stood upon the sand of the sea, and saw a beast rise up out of the sea, having seven heads and ten horns, and upon his horns ten crowns, and upon his heads the name of blasphemy.

2 And the beast which I saw was like unto a leopard, and his feet were as the feet of a bear, and his mouth as the mouth of a lion: and the dragon gave him his power, and his seat, and great authority.

3 And I saw one of his heads as it were wounded to death; and his deadly wound was healed: and all the world wondered after the beast.

4 And they worshipped the dragon which gave power unto the beast: and they worshipped the beast, saying, Who is like unto the beast? who is able to make war with him?

5 And there was given unto him a mouth speaking great things and blasphemies; and power was given unto him to continue forty and two months.

6 And he opened his mouth in blasphemy against God, to blaspheme his name, and his tabernacle, and them that dwell in heaven.

7 And it was given unto him to make war with the saints, and to overcome them: and power was given him over all kindreds, and tongues, and nations.

8 And all that dwell upon the earth shall worship him, whose names are not written in the book of life of the Lamb slain from the foundation of the world.

9 If any man have an ear, let him hear.

10 He that leadeth into captivity shall go into captivity: he that killeth with the sword must be killed with the sword. Here is the patience and the faith of the saints.

11 And I beheld another beast coming up out of the earth; and he had two horns like a lamb, and he spake as a dragon.

12 And he exerciseth all the power of the first beast before him, and causeth the earth and them which dwell therein to worship the first beast, whose deadly wound was healed.

13 And he doeth great wonders, so that he maketh fire come down from heaven on the earth in the sight of men,

14 And deceiveth them that dwell on the earth by the means of those miracles which he had power to do in the sight of the beast; saying to them that dwell on the earth, that they should make an image to the beast, which had the wound by a sword, and did live.

15 And he had power to give life unto the image of the beast, that the image of the beast should both speak, and cause that as many as would not worship the image of the beast should be killed.

16 And he causeth all, both small and great, rich and poor, free and bond, to receive a mark in their right hand, or in their foreheads:

17 And that no man might buy or sell, save he that had the mark, or the name of the beast, or the number of his name.

18 Here is wisdom. Let him that hath understanding count the number of the beast: for it is the number of a man; and his number is Six hundred threescore and six.

Chapter 14

1 And I looked, and, lo, a Lamb stood on the mount Sion, and with him an hundred forty and four thousand, having his Father's name written in their foreheads.

2 And I heard a voice from heaven, as the voice of many waters, and as the voice of a great thunder: and I heard the voice of harpers harping with their harps:

3 And they sung as it were a new song before the throne, and before the four beasts, and the elders: and no man could learn that song but the hundred and forty and four thousand, which were redeemed from the earth.

4 These are they which were not defiled with women; for they are virgins. These are they which follow the Lamb whithersoever he goeth. These were redeemed from among men, being the firstfruits unto God and to the Lamb.

5 And in their mouth was found no guile: for they are without fault before the throne of God.

6 And I saw another angel fly in the midst of heaven, having the everlasting gospel to preach unto them that dwell on the earth, and to every nation, and kindred, and tongue, and people,

7 Saying with a loud voice, Fear God, and give glory to him; for the hour of his judgment is come: and worship him that made heaven, and earth, and the sea, and the fountains of waters.

8 And there followed another angel, saying, Babylon is fallen, is fallen, that great city, because she made all nations drink of the wine of the wrath of her fornication.

9 And the third angel followed them, saying with a loud voice, If any man worship the beast and his image, and receive his mark in his forehead, or in his hand,

10 The same shall drink of the wine of the wrath of God, which is poured out without mixture into the cup of his indignation; and he shall be tormented with fire and brimstone in the presence of the holy angels, and in the presence of the Lamb:

11 And the smoke of their torment ascendeth up for ever and ever: and they have no rest day nor night, who worship the beast and his image, and whosoever receiveth the mark of his name.

12 Here is the patience of the saints: here are they that keep the commandments of God, and the faith of Jesus.

13 And I heard a voice from heaven saying unto me, Write, Blessed are the dead which die in the Lord from henceforth: Yea, saith the

Spirit, that they may rest from their labours; and their works do follow them.

14 And I looked, and behold a white cloud, and upon the cloud one sat like unto the Son of man, having on his head a golden crown, and in his hand a sharp sickle.

15 And another angel came out of the temple, crying with a loud voice to him that sat on the cloud, Thrust in thy sickle, and reap: for the time is come for thee to reap; for the harvest of the earth is ripe.

16 And he that sat on the cloud thrust in his sickle on the earth; and the earth was reaped.

17 And another angel came out of the temple which is in heaven, he also having a sharp sickle.

18 And another angel came out from the altar, which had power over fire; and cried with a loud cry to him that had the sharp sickle, saying, Thrust in thy sharp sickle, and gather the clusters of the vine of the earth; for her grapes are fully ripe.

19 And the angel thrust in his sickle into the earth, and gathered the vine of the earth, and cast it into the great winepress of the wrath of God.

20 And the winepress was trodden without the city, and blood came out of the winepress, even unto the horse bridles, by the space of a thousand and six hundred furlongs.

Chapter 15

1 And I saw another sign in heaven, great and marvellous, seven angels having the seven last plagues; for in them is filled up the wrath of God.

2 And I saw as it were a sea of glass mingled with fire: and them that had gotten the victory over the beast, and over his image, and over his mark, and over the number of his name, stand on the sea of glass, having the harps of God.

3 And they sing the song of Moses the servant of God, and the song of the Lamb, saying, Great and marvellous are thy works, Lord God Almighty; just and true are thy ways, thou King of saints.

4 Who shall not fear thee, O Lord, and glorify thy name? for thou only art holy: for all nations shall come and worship before thee; for thy judgments are made manifest.

5 And after that I looked, and, behold, the temple of the tabernacle of the testimony in heaven was opened:

6 And the seven angels came out of the temple, having the seven plagues, clothed in pure and white linen, and having their breasts girded with golden girdles.

7 And one of the four beasts gave unto the seven angels seven golden vials full of the wrath of God, who liveth for ever and ever.

8 And the temple was filled with smoke from the glory of God, and from his power; and no man was able to enter into the temple, till the seven plagues of the seven angels were fulfilled.

Chapter 16

1 And I heard a great voice out of the temple saying to the seven angels, Go your ways, and pour out the vials of the wrath of God upon the earth.

2 And the first went, and poured out his vial upon the earth; and there fell a noisome and grievous sore upon the men which had the mark of the beast, and upon them which worshipped his image.

3 And the second angel poured out his vial upon the sea; and it became as the blood of a dead man: and every living soul died in the sea.

4 And the third angel poured out his vial upon the rivers and fountains of waters; and they became blood.

5 And I heard the angel of the waters say, Thou art righteous, O Lord, which art, and wast, and shalt be, because thou hast judged thus.

6 For they have shed the blood of saints and prophets, and thou hast given them blood to drink; for they are worthy.

7 And I heard another out of the altar say, Even so, Lord God Almighty, true and righteous are thy judgments.

8 And the fourth angel poured out his vial upon the sun; and power was given unto him to scorch men with fire.

9 And men were scorched with great heat, and blasphemed the name of God, which hath power over these plagues: and they repented not to give him glory.

10 And the fifth angel poured out his vial upon the seat of the beast; and his kingdom was full of darkness; and they gnawed their tongues for pain,

11 And blasphemed the God of heaven because of their pains and their sores, and repented not of their deeds.

12 And the sixth angel poured out his vial upon the great river Euphrates; and the water thereof was dried up, that the way of the kings of the east might be prepared.

13 And I saw three unclean spirits like frogs come out of the mouth of the dragon, and out of the mouth of the beast, and out of the mouth of the false prophet.

14 For they are the spirits of devils, working miracles, which go forth unto the kings of the earth and of the whole world, to gather them to the battle of that great day of God Almighty.

15 Behold, I come as a thief. Blessed is he that watcheth, and keepeth his garments, lest he walk naked, and they see his shame.

16 And he gathered them together into a place called in the Hebrew tongue Armageddon.

17 And the seventh angel poured out his vial into the air; and there came a great voice out of the temple of heaven, from the throne, saying, It is done.

18 And there were voices, and thunders, and lightnings; and there was a great earthquake, such as was not since men were upon the earth, so mighty an earthquake, and so great.

19 And the great city was divided into three parts, and the cities of the nations fell: and great Babylon came in remembrance before God, to give unto her the cup of the wine of the fierceness of his wrath.

20 And every island fled away, and the mountains were not found.

21 And there fell upon men a great hail out of heaven, every stone about the weight of a talent: and men blasphemed God because of the plague of the hail; for the plague thereof was exceeding great.

Chapter 17

1 And there came one of the seven angels which had the seven vials, and talked with me, saying unto me, Come hither; I will shew unto thee the judgment of the great whore that sitteth upon many waters:

2 With whom the kings of the earth have committed fornication, and the inhabitants of the earth have been made drunk with the wine of her fornication.

3 So he carried me away in the spirit into the wilderness: and I saw a woman sit upon a scarlet coloured beast, full of names of blasphemy, having seven heads and ten horns.

4 And the woman was arrayed in purple and scarlet colour, and decked with gold and precious stones and pearls, having a golden cup in her hand full of abominations and filthiness of her fornication:

5 And upon her forehead was a name written, MYSTERY, BABYLON THE GREAT, THE MOTHER OF HARLOTS AND ABOMINATIONS OF THE EARTH.

6 And I saw the woman drunken with the blood of the saints, and with the blood of the martyrs of Jesus: and when I saw her, I wondered with great admiration.

7 And the angel said unto me, Wherefore didst thou marvel? I will tell thee the mystery of the woman, and of the beast that carrieth her, which hath the seven heads and ten horns.

8 The beast that thou sawest was, and is not; and shall ascend out of the bottomless pit, and go into perdition: and they that dwell on the earth shall wonder, whose names were not written in the book of life from the foundation of the world, when they behold the beast that was, and is not, and yet is.

9 And here is the mind which hath wisdom. The seven heads are seven mountains, on which the woman sitteth.

10 And there are seven kings: five are fallen, and one is, and the other is not yet come; and when he cometh, he must continue a short space.

11 And the beast that was, and is not, even he is the eighth, and is of the seven, and goeth into perdition.

12 And the ten horns which thou sawest are ten kings, which have received no kingdom as yet; but receive power as kings one hour with the beast.

13 These have one mind, and shall give their power and strength unto the beast.

14 These shall make war with the Lamb, and the Lamb shall overcome them: for he is Lord of lords, and King of kings: and they that are with him are called, and chosen, and faithful.

15 And he saith unto me, The waters which thou sawest, where the whore sitteth, are peoples, and multitudes, and nations, and tongues.

16 And the ten horns which thou sawest upon the beast, these shall hate the whore, and shall make her desolate and naked, and shall eat her flesh, and burn her with fire.

17 For God hath put in their hearts to fulfil his will, and to agree, and give their kingdom unto the beast, until the words of God shall be fulfilled.

18 And the woman which thou sawest is that great city, which reigneth over the kings of the earth.

Chapter 18

1 And after these things I saw another angel come down from heaven, having great power; and the earth was lightened with his glory.

2 And he cried mightily with a strong voice, saying, Babylon the great is fallen, is fallen, and is become the habitation of devils, and the hold of every foul spirit, and a cage of every unclean and hateful bird.

3 For all nations have drunk of the wine of the wrath of her fornication, and the kings of the earth have committed fornication with her, and the merchants of the earth are waxed rich through the abundance of her delicacies.

4 And I heard another voice from heaven, saying, Come out of her, my people, that ye be not partakers of her sins, and that ye receive not of her plagues.

5 For her sins have reached unto heaven, and God hath remembered her iniquities.

6 Reward her even as she rewarded you, and double unto her double according to her works: in the cup which she hath filled fill to her double.

7 How much she hath glorified herself, and lived deliciously, so much torment and sorrow give her: for she saith in her heart, I sit a queen, and am no widow, and shall see no sorrow.

8 Therefore shall her plagues come in one day, death, and mourning, and famine; and she shall be utterly burned with fire: for strong is the Lord God who judgeth her.

9 And the kings of the earth, who have committed fornication and lived deliciously with her, shall bewail her, and lament for her, when they shall see the smoke of her burning,

10 Standing afar off for the fear of her torment, saying, Alas, alas, that great city Babylon, that mighty city! for in one hour is thy judgment come.

11 And the merchants of the earth shall weep and mourn over her; for no man buyeth their merchandise any more:

12 The merchandise of gold, and silver, and precious stones, and of pearls, and fine linen, and purple, and silk, and scarlet, and all thyine wood, and all manner vessels of ivory, and all manner vessels of most precious wood, and of brass, and iron, and marble,

13 And cinnamon, and odours, and ointments, and frankincense, and wine, and oil, and fine flour, and wheat, and beasts, and sheep, and horses, and chariots, and slaves, and souls of men.

14 And the fruits that thy soul lusted after are departed from thee, and all things which were dainty and goodly are departed from thee, and thou shalt find them no more at all.

15 The merchants of these things, which were made rich by her, shall stand afar off for the fear of her torment, weeping and wailing,

16 And saying, Alas, alas, that great city, that was clothed in fine linen, and purple, and scarlet, and decked with gold, and precious stones, and pearls!

17 For in one hour so great riches is come to nought. And every ship-master, and all the company in ships, and sailors, and as many as trade by sea, stood afar off,

18 And cried when they saw the smoke of her burning, saying, What city is like unto this great city!

19 And they cast dust on their heads, and cried, weeping and wailing, saying, Alas, alas, that great city, wherein were made rich all that had ships in the sea by reason of her costliness! for in one hour is she made desolate.

20 Rejoice over her, thou heaven, and ye holy apostles and prophets; for God hath avenged you on her.

21 And a mighty angel took up a stone like a great millstone, and cast it into the sea, saying, Thus with violence shall that great city Babylon be thrown down, and shall be found no more at all.

22 And the voice of harpers, and musicians, and of pipers, and trumpeters, shall be heard no more at all in thee; and no craftsman, of whatsoever craft he be, shall be found any more in thee; and the sound of a millstone shall be heard no more at all in thee;

23 And the light of a candle shall shine no more at all in thee; and the voice of the bridegroom and of the bride shall be heard no more at all in thee: for thy merchants were the great men of the earth; for by thy sorceries were all nations deceived.

24 And in her was found the blood of prophets, and of saints, and of all that were slain upon the earth.

Chapter 19

1 And after these things I heard a great voice of much people in heaven, saying, Alleluia; Salvation, and glory, and honour, and power, unto the Lord our God:

2 For true and righteous are his judgments: for he hath judged the great whore, which did corrupt the earth with her fornication, and hath avenged the blood of his servants at her hand.

3 And again they said, Alleluia. And her smoke rose up for ever and ever.

4 And the four and twenty elders and the four beasts fell down and worshipped God that sat on the throne, saying, Amen; Alleluia.

5 And a voice came out of the throne, saying, Praise our God, all ye his servants, and ye that fear him, both small and great.

6 And I heard as it were the voice of a great multitude, and as the voice of many waters, and as the voice of mighty thunderings, saying, Alleluia: for the Lord God omnipotent reigneth.

7 Let us be glad and rejoice, and give honour to him: for the marriage of the Lamb is come, and his wife hath made herself ready.

8 And to her was granted that she should be arrayed in fine linen, clean and white: for the fine linen is the righteousness of saints.

9 And he saith unto me, Write, Blessed are they which are called unto the marriage supper of the Lamb. And he saith unto me, These are the true sayings of God.

10 And I fell at his feet to worship him. And he said unto me, See thou do it not: I am thy fellowservant, and of thy brethren that have the testimony of Jesus: worship God: for the testimony of Jesus is the spirit of prophecy.

11 And I saw heaven opened, and behold a white horse; and he that sat upon him was called Faithful and True, and in righteousness he doth judge and make war.

12 His eyes were as a flame of fire, and on his head were many crowns; and he had a name written, that no man knew, but he himself.

13 And he was clothed with a vesture dipped in blood: and his name is called The Word of God.

14 And the armies which were in heaven followed him upon white horses, clothed in fine linen, white and clean.

15 And out of his mouth goeth a sharp sword, that with it he should smite the nations: and he shall rule them with a rod of iron: and he treadeth the winepress of the fierceness and wrath of Almighty God.

16 And he hath on his vesture and on his thigh a name written, KING OF KINGS, AND LORD OF LORDS.

17 And I saw an angel standing in the sun; and he cried with a loud voice, saying to all the fowls that fly in the midst of heaven, Come and gather yourselves together unto the supper of the great God;

18 That ye may eat the flesh of kings, and the flesh of captains, and the flesh of mighty men, and the flesh of horses, and of them that sit on them, and the flesh of all men, both free and bond, both small and great.

19 And I saw the beast, and the kings of the earth, and their armies, gathered together to make war against him that sat on the horse, and against his army.

20 And the beast was taken, and with him the false prophet that wrought miracles before him, with which he deceived them that had received the mark of the beast, and them that worshipped his image. These both were cast alive into a lake of fire burning with brimstone.

21 And the remnant were slain with the sword of him that sat upon the horse, which sword proceeded out of his mouth: and all the fowls were filled with their flesh.

Chapter 20

1 And I saw an angel come down from heaven, having the key of the bottomless pit and a great chain in his hand.

2 And he laid hold on the dragon, that old serpent, which is the Devil, and Satan, and bound him a thousand years,

3 And cast him into the bottomless pit, and shut him up, and set a seal upon him, that he should deceive the nations no more, till the thousand years should be fulfilled: and after that he must be loosed a little season.

4 And I saw thrones, and they sat upon them, and judgment was given unto them: and I saw the souls of them that were beheaded for the witness of Jesus, and for the word of God, and which had not worshipped the beast, neither his image, neither had received his mark upon their foreheads, or in their hands; and they lived and reigned with Christ a thousand years.

5 But the rest of the dead lived not again until the thousand years were finished. This is the first resurrection.

6 Blessed and holy is he that hath part in the first resurrection: on such the second death hath no power, but they shall be priests of God and of Christ, and shall reign with him a thousand years.

7 And when the thousand years are expired, Satan shall be loosed out of his prison,

8 And shall go out to deceive the nations which are in the four quarters of the earth, Gog and Magog, to gather them together to battle: the number of whom is as the sand of the sea.

9 And they went up on the breadth of the earth, and compassed the camp of the saints about, and the beloved city: and fire came down from God out of heaven, and devoured them.

10 And the devil that deceived them was cast into the lake of fire and brimstone, where the beast and the false prophet are, and shall be tormented day and night for ever and ever.

11 And I saw a great white throne, and him that sat on it, from whose face the earth and the heaven fled away; and there was found no place for them.

12 And I saw the dead, small and great, stand before God; and the books were opened: and another book was opened, which is the book of life: and the dead were judged out of those things which were written in the books, according to their works.

13 And the sea gave up the dead which were in it; and death and hell delivered up the dead which were in them: and they were judged every man according to their works.

14 And death and hell were cast into the lake of fire. This is the second death.

15 And whosoever was not found written in the book of life was cast into the lake of fire.

Chapter 21

1 And I saw a new heaven and a new earth: for the first heaven and the first earth were passed away; and there was no more sea.

2 And I John saw the holy city, new Jerusalem, coming down from God out of heaven, prepared as a bride adorned for her husband.

3 And I heard a great voice out of heaven saying, Behold, the tabernacle of God is with men, and he will dwell with them, and they shall be his people, and God himself shall be with them, and be their God.

4 And God shall wipe away all tears from their eyes; and there shall be no more death, neither sorrow, nor crying, neither shall there be any more pain: for the former things are passed away.

5 And he that sat upon the throne said, Behold, I make all things new. And he said unto me, Write: for these words are true and faithful.

6 And he said unto me, It is done. I am Alpha and Omega, the beginning and the end. I will give unto him that is athirst of the fountain of the water of life freely.

7 He that overcometh shall inherit all things; and I will be his God, and he shall be my son.

8 But the fearful, and unbelieving, and the abominable, and murderers, and whoremongers, and sorcerers, and idolaters, and all liars, shall have their part in the lake which burneth with fire and brimstone: which is the second death.

9 And there came unto me one of the seven angels which had the seven vials full of the seven last plagues, and talked with me, saying, Come hither, I will shew thee the bride, the Lamb's wife.

10 And he carried me away in the spirit to a great and high mountain, and shewed me that great city, the holy Jerusalem, descending out of heaven from God,

11 Having the glory of God: and her light was like unto a stone most precious, even like a jasper stone, clear as crystal;

12 And had a wall great and high, and had twelve gates, and at the gates twelve angels, and names written thereon, which are the names of the twelve tribes of the children of Israel:

13 On the east three gates; on the north three gates; on the south three gates; and on the west three gates.

14 And the wall of the city had twelve foundations, and in them the names of the twelve apostles of the Lamb.

15 And he that talked with me had a golden reed to measure the city, and the gates thereof, and the wall thereof.

16 And the city lieth foursquare, and the length is as large as the breadth: and he measured the city with the reed, twelve thousand furlongs. The length and the breadth and the height of it are equal.

17 And he measured the wall thereof, an hundred and forty and four cubits, according to the measure of a man, that is, of the angel.

18 And the building of the wall of it was of jasper: and the city was pure gold, like unto clear glass.

19 And the foundations of the wall of the city were garnished with all manner of precious stones. The first foundation was jasper; the second, sapphire; the third, a chalcedony; the fourth, an emerald;

20 The fifth, sardonyx; the sixth, sardius; the seventh, chrysolyte; the eighth, beryl; the ninth, a topaz; the tenth, a chrysoprasus; the eleventh, a jacinth; the twelfth, an amethyst.

21 And the twelve gates were twelve pearls; every several gate was of one pearl: and the street of the city was pure gold, as it were transparent glass.

22 And I saw no temple therein: for the Lord God Almighty and the Lamb are the temple of it.

23 And the city had no need of the sun, neither of the moon, to shine in it: for the glory of God did lighten it, and the Lamb is the light thereof.

24 And the nations of them which are saved shall walk in the light of it: and the kings of the earth do bring their glory and honour into it.

25 And the gates of it shall not be shut at all by day: for there shall be no night there.

26 And they shall bring the glory and honour of the nations into it.

27 And there shall in no wise enter into it any thing that defileth, neither whatsoever worketh abomination, or maketh a lie: but they which are written in the Lamb's book of life.

Chapter 22

1 And he shewed me a pure river of water of life, clear as crystal, proceeding out of the throne of God and of the Lamb.

2 In the midst of the street of it, and on either side of the river, was there the tree of life, which bare twelve manner of fruits, and yielded her fruit every month: and the leaves of the tree were for the healing of the nations.

3 And there shall be no more curse: but the throne of God and of the Lamb shall be in it; and his servants shall serve him:

4 And they shall see his face; and his name shall be in their foreheads.

5 And there shall be no night there; and they need no candle, neither light of the sun; for the Lord God giveth them light: and they shall reign for ever and ever.

6 And he said unto me, These sayings are faithful and true: and the Lord God of the holy prophets sent his angel to shew unto his servants the things which must shortly be done.

7 Behold, I come quickly: blessed is he that keepeth the sayings of the prophecy of this book.

8 And I John saw these things, and heard them. And when I had heard and seen, I fell down to worship before the feet of the angel which shewed me these things.

9 Then saith he unto me, See thou do it not: for I am thy fellowservant, and of thy brethren the prophets, and of them which keep the sayings of this book: worship God.

10 And he saith unto me, Seal not the sayings of the prophecy of this book: for the time is at hand.

11 He that is unjust, let him be unjust still: and he which is filthy, let him be filthy still: and he that is righteous, let him be righteous still: and he that is holy, let him be holy still.

12 And, behold, I come quickly; and my reward is with me, to give every man according as his work shall be.

13 I am Alpha and Omega, the beginning and the end, the first and the last.

14 Blessed are they that do his commandments, that they may have right to the tree of life, and may enter in through the gates into the city.

15 For without are dogs, and sorcerers, and whoremongers, and murderers, and idolaters, and whosoever loveth and maketh a lie.

16 I Jesus have sent mine angel to testify unto you these things in the churches. I am the root and the offspring of David, and the bright and morning star.

17 And the Spirit and the bride say, Come. And let him that heareth say, Come. And let him that is athirst come. And whosoever will, let him take the water of life freely.

18 For I testify unto every man that heareth the words of the prophecy of this book, If any man shall add unto these things, God shall add unto him the plagues that are written in this book:

19 And if any man shall take away from the words of the book of this prophecy, God shall take away his part out of the book of life, and out of the holy city, and from the things which are written in this book.

20 He which testifieth these things saith, Surely I come quickly. Amen. Even so, come, Lord Jesus.

21 The grace of our Lord Jesus Christ be with you all. Amen.

NOTES

Chapter 2—Who Left and Where Did They Go?

1. Hal Lindsey, *The Rapture* (New York: Bantam Books, 1983), pp. 36-38.

Chapter 3—Who Is This Great Leader?

1. Dave Breese, as quoted on *Left Behind: Where'd Everybody Go?*, a video produced by This Week in Bible Prophecy Ministry, 1994, Niagara Falls, NY.

2. J. Dwight Pentecost, *Things to Come*, Academie Books (Grand Rapids, MI: Zondervan Publishing House, 1964), pp. 204-05.

3. Associated Press, June 8, 1990.

4. Malachi Martin, *The Keys of This Blood* (New York: Simon and Schuster, 1990), p. 209.

Chapter 5—What Are Some of the Excuses You Will Hear?

1. *Deseret News*, Church Section, June 18, 1873, p. 308, as cited in Ed Decker and Dave Hunt, *The God Makers* (Eugene, OR: Harvest House Publishers, 1984), p. 30.

2. *The Journal of Holistic Health*, 1977, Jack Gibb, "Psycho-Sociological Aspects of Holistic Health," p. 44; as cited in Dave Hunt, *The Seduction of Christianity* (Eugene, OR: Harvest House Publishers, 1985), p. 119.

3. Werner Erhard, *If God Had Meant Man to Fly, He Would Have Given Him Wings*, p. 11.

4. Benjamin Creme, *The Reappearance of the Christ and the Masters of Wisdom* (London: The Tara Press, 1980), Message No. 81, Sept. 21, 1979, p. 246.

5. *Meditations of Maharishi Mahesh Yogi*, p. 178.

6. Sun Myung Moon, as quoted in Dave Hunt, *The Seduction of Christianity* (Eugene, OR: Harvest House Publishers, 1985), p. 56.

7. Willis Harman (New York: W. W. Norton & Co., 1976), p. 94.

8. Ken Wilber, *The Atman Project*; as cited in Dave Hunt and T.A. McMahon, *The Sorcerer's New Apprentice* (Eugene, OR: Harvest House Publishers, 1988), p. 227.

9. Barbara Marx Hubbard, *The Book of Co-Creation: An Evolutionary Interpretation of the New Testament*, a three-part unpublished manuscript dated 1980.

10. Andrew Lang, *Cleveland Plain Dealer* (Cleveland, OH: The Christic Institute), Jan. 4, 1989.

11. Barbara Marx Hubbard, *Book of Co-Creation*.

12. Ruth Montgomery, "Threshold to Tomorrow," *Magical Blend*, Issue 113, 1986, p. 206.

13. Barbara Marx Hubbard, *Happy Birth Day Planet Earth: The Instant of Cooperation* (Santa Fe, NM: Ocean Tree Books, 1986), pp. 12, 17, 19.

14. *UFOs: The Hidden Truth*, a video presentation by New Liberty Films and Video, Shawnee Mission, KS.

15. Ibid.

16. Jacques Vallee, *Messengers of Deception* (Berkeley, 1979), pp. 204-05; as cited in *The Cult Explosion*, Dave Hunt (Eugene. OR: Harvest House Publishers, 1980), pp. 19-20.

17. Jacques Vallee, *Dimensions: A Casebook of Alien Contact* (Chicago, IL: Contemporary Books, 1988), pp. 172-73.

18. Whitley Strieber, *Communion: A True Story*, (New York: Aron Books, 1987), pp. 4, 94.

19. Whitley Strieber, *Transformation: The Breakthrough* (New York: Beech Tree Books, 1988), pp. 225-26.

20. Jacques Vallee, *Dimensions*, p. 178.

21. Ibid., quote from foreword by Whitley Strieber.

22. Ibid., pp. 215-16.

Chapter 6—*Why You Shouldn't Take the Mark*

1. *Washington Times*, Oct. 13, 1993.

2. Terry Galanoy, *Charge It* (New York: Putnam Publishers, 1980).

Chapter 7—*Where Are You Now in History?*

1. Sir Robert Anderson, *The Coming Prince* (Grand Rapids, MI: Kregel Publications, 1984), pp. 121-22.

2. Ibid., pp. 127-28.

Chapter 8—*What's Going On in the Middle East?*

1. From Washington Declaration of July 25, 1994.

2. Benjamin Netanyahu, *A Place Among Nations* (New York: Bantam Books, 1993), p. 259.

N CASE OF RAPTURE, WATCH THIS VIDEO...

LEFT BEHIND
WHERE'D EVERYBODY GO?

Completely Revolutionary, Soul Winning Outreach

This exciting video is the first gospel video message that has ever been prepared specially for e who will be left behind after the Rapture takes place.

Most importantly, it will answer the questions that those left behind will be asking.

- Who left and where did they go?
- Who is the great leader that has arisen onto the world scene?
- What is the New World Order they are talking about?
- Why shouldn't I believe them with all the incredible powers they have?
- What is the mark of allegiance and why shouldn't I take it?
- What is going to happen next? What are my choices?

These are just some of the questions this powerful and exciting video will tackle. If you understand the power of the prophetic Word God, and if you have a loved one or friend who does not know the Lord, then you will understand power of what we have created in this soul-winning video *Left Behind... Where'd Everybody Go?*

A perfect complement to the book *Left Behind*.

ncludes a dramatic enactment of how events will take place after the Rapture!
Only $19.95 plus $3.50 S&H

Easy To Order
Call Now:
1-800-565-2413
(M-F, 9-5 Eastern Time)
Or Write To:
This Week In Bible Prophecy
P.O. Box 665, Niagara Falls, ON L2E 6V5
P.O. Box 1440, Niagara Falls, NY 14302-1440

RACING TOWARD...
THE MARK
OF THE BEAST VIDEO

Is a cashless society just around the corner? Is it possible to number and track ery person on earth, to monitor every purchase and sale? How close are we to a w World Order?

In this startling video, based on the best-selling book, prophecy experts and tural observers Peter and Paul Lalonde of "This Week In Bible Prophecy" detail azing new technological breakthroughs that are quickly paving the way to the radical onomic system predicted in Scripture. You will discover...

- HOW POWERFUL NEW IDENTIFICATION SYSTEMS CAN TRACK EVERY PERSON ON THE PLANET.
- HOW CASH IS BEING REPLACED BY ELECTRONIC ALTERNATIVES.
- HOW CONCERN ABOUT CRIME IS ACCELERATING PUBLIC ACCEPTANCE OF FORMERLY DISTRUSTED CASHLESS SYSTEMS.
- WHY *THIS* GENERATION, UNLIKE ANY BEFORE IT, IS CAPABLE OF FULFILLING CRUCIAL END-TIMES PROPHECIES.

Sifting fact from fiction and wild rumor from documented truth, Peter and Paul will ke you on an exhilarating trip into the near future— and point to the Lord Jesus hrist as the ultimate answer to the world's growing chaos.

The Christian World Report

If you're tired of getting your news on world events from sources who just don't understand your perspective; if you would like up-to-date, accurate information on how world events tie in with the Bible and today's Christian, this is definitely the news source for you. *The Christian World Report*, brought to you by *This Week In Bible Prophecy Ministries,* is *the* most accurate, up-to-date news source available. Eleven issues delivered to your door annually, each one covering world news and events from a Christian point of view, ensuring that you get the kinds of stories your local newspaper or evening news report are too afraid to tell.
Subscribe today for only $24.95

This Week In Bible Prophecy Magazine

Imagine a book on Bible prophecy that never ends. A book that can document and explain the fulfillments of prophecy with full color illustrations and in-depth analysis and insight. A book that is always exciting and always up-to-date, with a new chapter delivered to your door every single month. Well, you don't have

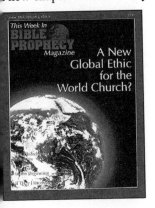

to imagine it any more. It's *This Week In Bible Prophecy Magazine*.
Pictures, maps, charts, interviews with experts from every field, and some of the most powerful and accurate research that you're going to find anywhere. You'll find it all in *This Week In Bible Prophecy Magazine*.
Subscribe today for only $29.95

Call Now:
1-800-565-2413
(M-F, 9-5 Eastern Time)

Or write to:
This Week In Bible Prophecy
P.O. Box 665,
Niagara Falls, ON L2E 6V5
P.O. Box 1440,
Niagara Falls, NY 14302-1440